WINDOWS™ 3.1

Lisa A. Bucki

alpha books

A Division of Prentice Hall Computer Publishing

11711 North College Avenue, Carmel, Indiana 46032 USA

© **1993 by Alpha Books**

All rights reserved. No part of this book shall be reproduced, stored in a retrieval system, or transmitted by any means, electronic, mechanical, photocopying, recording, or otherwise, without written permission from the publisher. No patent liability is assumed with respect to the use of the information contained herein. Although every precaution has been taken in the preparation of this book, the publisher and author assume no responsibility for errors or omissions. Neither is any liability assumed for damages resulting from the use of the information contained herein. For information, address Alpha Books, 11711 N. College Ave., Carmel, IN 46032.

International Standard Book Number: 1-56761-139-7
Library of Congress Catalog Card Number: 92-83850

95   7 6 5 4

Interpretation of the printing code: the rightmost number of the first series of numbers is the year of the book's printing; the rightmost number of the second series of numbers is the number of the book's printing. For example, a printing code of 93-1 shows that the first printing of the book occurred in 1993.

Publisher: *Marie Butler-Knight*
Managing Editor: *Elizabeth Keaffaber*
Acquisitions Manager: *Stephen R. Poland*
Development Editor: *Seta Frantz*
Production Editor: *Annalise N. Di Paolo*
Copy Editor: *Barry Childs-Helton*
Cover Designer: *Jay Corpus*
Designer: *Amy Peppler-Adams*
Indexers: *Jeanne Clark, Johnna VanHoose*
Production Team: *Tim Cox, Mark Enochs, Tim Groeling, Phil Kitchel, Tom Loveman, Joe Ramon, Carrie Roth, Kelli Widdifield*

Special thanks to Margaret Colvin for ensuring the technical accuracy of this book.

Screen reproductions in this book were created by means of the program Collage Plus from Inner Media, Inc., Hollis, NH.

Printed in the United States of America

Contents

Introduction vii
Windows Basics ix

Applications—Installing 1
Applications—Switching 3

Clipboard—Changing Format 5
Clipboard—Cutting or Copying to 6
Clipboard—Deleting Contents 8
Clipboard—Opening a File 9
Clipboard—Pasting from 10
Clipboard—Saving Contents 11
Clipboard—Starting the
 Clipboard Viewer 13
Colors—Changing for
 a Screen Element 14
Colors—Choosing a New Scheme 16
Colors—Creating Custom 17
Colors—Opening
 the Color Dialog Box 19

Desktop—Arranging 20
Desktop—Customizing 20
Directories—Creating 23
Directories—Viewing 25
Directory Tree—Expanding Levels 26
Directory Tree—Selecting Drives
 and Directories 28
Directory Window—Arranging 29
Directory Window—Closing 30
Directory Window—Moving the Split ... 30
Directory Window—Opening
 Additional 31

Directory Window—Refreshing
the File List 32
Disk— Copying 33
Disk—Formatting 36
DOS Applications—Changing
Settings 39
DOS Fonts—Changing 42
Drivers—Adding for Sound
and Video 44
Drivers—Selecting for Video 48

File Manager—Options 50
File Manager—Starting 52
Files—Associating 53
Files—Copying 55
Files—Deleting 58
Files—Moving 60
Files—Renaming 62
Files—Running 65
Files—Searching for 67
Files—Selecting 69
Files—Viewing 70
Fonts—Adding 75
Fonts—Removing 78

Hardware Settings 80
Help 82

Icons—Arranging 85
Icons—Selecting 86

International Options 87

Keyboard—Modifying 90

Links—Creating 92
Links—Updating 93

Mode—386 Enhanced Options 95
Mouse—Customizing 98

Objects—Embedding 100
Objects—Updating Embedded 102

PIF Editor—386 Enhanced Mode 104
PIF Editor—Standard Mode 109
Printers—Configuring 113
Printers—Selecting Default 116
Printers—Selecting Ports 117
Printing—Deleting a Job 119
Printing—Files 120
Printing—Pausing a Job 121
Printing—Priorities 122
Printing—Resuming a Job 123
Program Groups—Adding 124
Program Groups—Deleting 126
Program Manager—Options 127
Program Items—Adding 128
Program Items—Deleting 133
Program Items—Moving 135
Programs—Quitting 136
Programs—Starting 137
Properties—Files 138
Properties—Program 141

Serial Ports—Configuring 145
Sound—Configuring 147

Task List 150
TrueType—Setting Options 151

Windows—Arranging 152
Windows—Closing 153
Windows—Maximizing 154
Windows—Minimizing 155

Windows—Moving 156
Windows—Restoring 157
Windows—Selecting 158
Windows—Sizing 158

Index 161

Introduction

The One Minute Windows 3.1 Reference offers unique help when you are in a hurry with short and clear step-by-step instructions. This book is designed for the person who:

- Doesn't have time to flip through a large manual.

- Only wants the necessary steps to accomplish a task and not a lot of text.

- Wants no-nonsense instructions to complete a task.

The One Minute Windows 3.1 Reference explains the tasks you need to accomplish quickly in easy-to-understand steps.

Conventions Used In This Book

This book offers several features that will make using Windows 3.1 as simple as possible. These features include the following:

Windows tasks are organized in alphabetical order for quick and easy fingertip access to important Windows topics.

All steps are concise, with the keys you need to press or information you need to type to accomplish a task listed to the right of each step.

Keys to press are shown
as *keycaps* like this .... ⏎

Information to type is shown
in bold italic text like this .... ***text***

(Optional) Some steps may begin with **(Optional)**. If you do not wish to use this option, bypass the option.

Ctrl + or **Alt** +   These are key combinations used to accomplish a Windows task. For example, if you are asked to press **Alt** + **A**, press the **Alt** key and the **A** at the same time.

"OR"   If you see an "or" in a step, you can use the option of your choice in the step.

Some steps will take more than one keypress or action. When this is the case, you'll see the actions listed vertically .... **Alt** + **F**
⏎

This icon points out extra information and techniques Windows 3.1 features you may find valuable for using the program.

This icon gives examples on how to use the feature being discussed for better understanding.

Windows Basics

Microsoft Windows is an interface program that makes your computer easier to use; you select menu items and pictures rather than typing commands. It also lets you display each application in a ***window***, an area of the screen you can move and resize. Before you can take advantage of Windows, however, you must learn some Windows basics.

Starting Microsoft Windows

To start Windows, do the following:

1. At the DOS prompt, type .... **win**

2. Press .... ⏎

The Windows title screen appears for a few moments, and then the Windows ***desktop*** (the background) and the Program Manager (which lets you organize and start programs) appears. (See Figure 1.)

> ***What If It Didn't Work?*** *You may have to change to the windows directory before starting Windows; to do so, type **CD \WINDOWS** and press **Enter.***

Parts of a Windows Screen

The Windows screen contains several distinctive elements you won't see in DOS. Here's a brief summary.

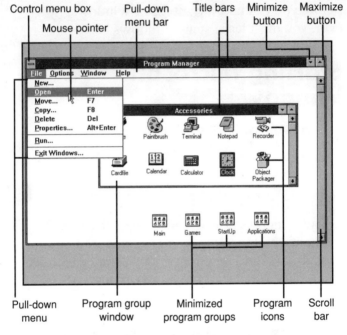

Figure 1   The Windows Program Manager.

- **Title bar**   Located along the top of a window or screen; shows the name of the window or program.

- **Program group window**   Contains program-item icons which allow you to run programs; can also be minimized (shrunk) to program group icons, which look like a small program group window.

- **Icons**   Graphic representations of programs, groups of programs, and special screen functions. To run a program, you select its program-item icon.

- **Minimize and Maximize buttons**
Located at the upper right corner of a window or screen, these look like a down arrow and up arrow; they alter a window's size. The Minimize button shrinks the window to the size of an icon. The Maximize button expands the window to fill the screen. When maximized, a window contains a double-arrow Restore button, which returns the window to its original size.

- **Control menu box**   Located in the upper left corner of a window or screen; looks like a box with a hyphen in it. When selected, pulls down a menu that offers size and location controls for the window.

- **Pull-down menu bar**   Located below the title bar; contains a list of the pull-down menus available in the program.

- **Mouse pointer**   Appears on-screen (usually as an arrow) if you are using a mouse. Control it by moving the mouse.

Windows Basics

- **Scroll bars**   These appear (usually at the bottom or right side of a window, or both) if a window contains more information than it can display. Scroll arrows on each end of the scroll bar allow you to scroll slowly. The scroll box allows you to scroll more quickly.

Using a Mouse

To work most efficiently in Windows, you should use a mouse. You can press mouse buttons and move the mouse in various ways to change the way it acts:

Point means to move the mouse pointer onto the specified item by moving the mouse. The tip of the mouse pointer must be touching the item.

Click on an item means to move the pointer onto the specified item, and press the mouse button once. Unless specified otherwise, use the left mouse button.

Double-click on an item means to move the pointer onto the specified item, and press and release the mouse button twice quickly.

Drag means to move the mouse pointer onto the specified item, hold down the mouse button, and move the mouse while holding down the button.

Choosing Menus and Commands

The **pull-down menu bar** contains various menus from which you can select commands. Each Windows application you run has a set of pull-down menus; Windows itself has a set. Each menu name, and the commands on the menu, have an underlined letter. This is the **selection letter** you can press to choose the menu or command with the keyboard. (Selection letters are indicated in bold in this book.) To open a menu and choose a command, use the steps described next.

Keyboard Steps

1. Choose the menu ... Alt + *selection letter*
2. Choose the command ....*selection letter*

Mouse Steps

1. Click on the menu name on the menu bar.
2. Click on the desired command.

> **TIP** *Notice that some commands are followed by key names such as **Enter** (for the Open command) or **F8** (for the Copy command). These are called **accelerator keys**. You can use these keys to perform these commands without even opening the menu.*

Windows Basics

Usually, when you select a command, the command is performed immediately. However:

- If the command name is *gray* (rather than black), the command is unavailable at the moment, and you cannot choose it.

- If the command name is followed by an *arrow*, selecting the command will cause another menu to appear, from which you select another command.

- If the command name is followed by an *ellipsis* (three dots), selecting it will cause a dialog box to appear. You'll learn about dialog boxes in the next section.

Navigating Dialog Boxes

A **dialog box** is Windows' way of requesting additional information. Each dialog box contains one or more of the following elements:

- *List boxes* display available choices. To activate a list, click inside the list box. If the entire list is not visible, use the scroll bar to view the items in the list. To select an item from the list, click on it.

- *Drop-down lists* are similar to list boxes, but only one item in the list is shown. To see the rest of the items, click on the down arrow to the right of the list box. To select an item from the list, click on it.

- *Text boxes* allow you to type an entry. To activate a text box, click inside it. To edit an existing entry, use the **arrow** keys to move the cursor, and the **Del** or **Backspace** keys to delete existing characters, and then type your correction.

- *Check boxes* allow you to select one or more items in a group of options. For example, if you are styling text, you may select Bold and Italic to have the text appear in both bold and italic type. Click on a check box to activate it.

- *Option buttons* are like check boxes, but you can select only one option button in a group. Selecting one button *deselects* any option that is already selected. Click on an option button to activate it.

- *Command buttons* execute (or cancel) the command once you have made your selections in the dialog box. To press a command button, click on it.

Applications—Installing

*The Windows Setup **applet** (small application) searches your system for installed applications, and presents a list of them. Choose which ones you want to run from Windows; Setup then creates Windows **program-item** icons for them. If Setup doesn't find an application, you can add it manually. See "Program Items—Adding."*

Keyboard Steps

1. Highlight the Main program group at the Program Manager ...... [Ctrl] + [Tab]

*You may have to press **Ctrl+Tab** several times to highlight the Main group icon.*

2. Press .... [↵]

3. Highlight the Windows Setup icon. .... [←], [→], [↑], or [↓]

4. Press .... [↵]

5. Choose the Options menu .... [Alt] + [O]

6. Choose Set Up Applications .... [S]

7. With the **Search for applications** option button selected, press .... [↵]

Applications—Installing 1

8. Select whether to search
   the Path or the drive ....

TIP *Windows may ask you to specify a name for some of the programs it finds. Highlight the correct program name and press **Enter** to continue the search.*

9. Move to the list of
   Applications found on
   hard disk(s) .... F

10. Select each application
    to install .... ↑ or ↓

    Space

    and select Add .... A
    or select Add All .... D

11. Press .... ↵

12. Choose the Options menu .... Alt + O

13. Choose Exit X

TIP *To install a specific application, select the **Ask you to specify an application** option button in step 7. Fill in the Application Path and Filename text box (by typing something like **c:\dos\ undelete.exe**). Or, choose the Browse button to find the file name. Choose the program group to which you want to add the program-item, then press **Enter** or click on **OK** to continue.*

2 Applications—Installing

Mouse Steps

1. At the Program Manager, double-click on the Main program group icon.
2. Double-click on the Windows Setup program-item icon.
3. Click on the **O**ptions menu.
4. Click on **S**earch for Applications.
5. Click on **OK**.
6. Click on either the **Path** or **Drive** option.
7. Click on **S**earch Now.
8. Click on each application to install from the list of Applications found.
9. Click on **A**dd or **A**dd All.
10. Click on **OK**.
11. Click on the **O**ptions menu.
12. Click on E**x**it.

Applications—Switching

Changes the active (top) application, so that you can move to the application you want to work in. You can use either the Task List or Control menu to move among applications, though you must use the keyboard to display the Task list.

*You can press **Alt+Esc** to cycle through the applications that are running (either in an open window or reduced to an icon). When an icon name is highlighted, press **Enter** to restore the application.*

Using the Task List to Switch Applications

1. To display the Task List, press .... `Ctrl` + `Esc`
2. Highlight the application you want to use .... `↑` or `↓`
3. To open the application, press .... `←`

 You also can click on an application with your mouse to highlight it in the Task List, then click on the Switch To command button to move to the application. Or simply double-click on the application name in the list to move to it.

Using the Control Menu to Switch Applications—Keyboard Steps

1. To display the Control menu, press .... `Alt` + `Space`
2. To display the Task List, choose Switch To .... `W`
3. Highlight the application you want to use .... `↑` or `↓`

Applications—Switching

4. To open the application, press .... ⏎

Using the Control Menu to Switch Applications—Mouse Steps

1. At the Application, click on the Control menu icon (upper left corner).

2. Click on **Switch To**.

3. Double-click on the application name.

Clipboard—Changing Format

*You can use the Clipboard Viewer's **Display** menu to change the format in which the Clipboard displays information. This lets you tell how the Clipboard contents will look when pasted into a different type of application. Of the three choices available, the formats you can't select are dimmed. Auto displays the text in its original format. **Text** formats the material for most Windows applications. Choose the **OEM** Text format for DOS applications. Bitmap changes the graphic displayed to a bitmapped format. (Other formats are available, depending on the material pasted to the Clipboard.)*

Keyboard Steps

1. Start the Clipboard Viewer from the Main program group. (See "Clipboard—Starting the Clipboard Viewer.")

2. Pull down the **Display** menu .... Alt + D

Clipboard—Changing Format 5

3. Choose a format:

   Auto .... [A]

   Text .... [T]

   OEM Text .... [O]

   Bitmap .... [B]

The Auto choice on the Clipboard Viewer's Display restores the original format of the Clipboard contents.

Mouse Steps

1. Start the Clipboard Viewer from the Main program group.
2. Click on the **D**isplay menu.
3. Click on a format:

   Auto

   Text

   OEM Text

   Bitmap

Clipboard—Cutting or Copying to

Storing material in the Clipboard is generally a matter of using one of two Edit menu commands—Copy or Cut. (For DOS applications, consult the documentation to learn whether or not you can cut to the Windows Clipboard when running Windows in 386 Enhanced mode.)

The Edit Copy command places a copy of the highlighted material into the Clipboard. Edit Cut deletes the highlighted material from its present location and puts it in the Clipboard.

Keyboard Steps

1. From a Windows application, select (highlight) the text or graphic you want in the Clipboard.
2. Pull down the Edit menu .... [Alt] + [E]
3. Choose Copy or Cut .... [C] or [T]

Whenever you cut or copy something to the Clipboard, it replaces anything that's currently in the Clipboard.

Mouse Steps

1. From a Windows application, select (highlight) the text or graphic you want in the Clipboard.
2. Click on the Edit menu.
3. Click on Copy or Cut.

Clipboard—Cutting or Copying to

Clipboard—Deleting Contents

Deleting the Clipboard contents empties the Clipboard. Nothing new is stored there (as when you Cut or Copy material).

Keyboard Steps

1. Start the Clipboard Viewer from the Main program group.

2. Pull down the Edit menu .... Alt + E

3. Choose Delete .... D

TIP

Pressing the Delete key is a shortcut for steps 2 and 3.

4. Choose Yes to confirm the deletion .... Y or ↵

Mouse Steps

1. Start the Clipboard Viewer from the Main program group.

2. Click on the Edit menu.

3. Click on Delete.

4. To continue, click on Yes.

*Pressing Esc doesn't cancel the operation. To cancel, press **N** or click on **No** at the Clear Clipboard dialog box.*

Clipboard—Opening a File

You can open any file you've previously saved from the Clipboard Viewer. Such a file has a .CLP extension. You can't open any other file type in the Viewer.

Keyboard Steps

1. Start the Clipboard Viewer from the Main program group.
2. Pull down the **F**ile menu .... `Alt` + `F`
3. Choose **O**pen .... `O`
4. Choose the **D**irectory list .... `Alt` + `D`
5. Highlight and select the directory containing the file you want to open .... `↑` or `↓`
   `↵`
6. Move to the File **N**ame list .... `Alt` + `N`
   `Tab`
7. Highlight and select the file you want to open .... `↑` or `↓`

8. Press .... ⏎

9. If you see the Clear Clipboard dialog box, press .... ⏎

TIP

If you clear the Clipboard before saving its contents, those contents are permanently deleted. Press N or click on No to go back to the Viewer. Then use the File Save As command to save.

Mouse Steps

1. Start the Clipboard Viewer from the Main program group.

2. Click on the File menu.

3. Click on Open.

4. Double-click on the directory with the file you want to open in the Directory list.

5. Double-click on the file you want to open in the File Name list.

6. If you see the Clear Clipboard dialog box, click on Yes.

Clipboard—Pasting from

Once you've cut or copied text or a graphic to the Clipboard, you can place it anywhere in a document for a Windows application using the following steps. (Pasting to a DOS application may be slightly different. See the documentation for the DOS application.)

Use the Paste Special command from the Edit menu to create a link between the document you're pasting into and the application where you originally created the Clipboard contents.

Keyboard Steps

1. Move the cursor in the document to the location where you want to insert the Clipboard contents.
2. Pull down the Edit menu .... Alt + E
3. Choose Paste .... P

Mouse Steps

1. Move the cursor in the document to the location where you want to insert the Clipboard contents.
2. Click on the Edit menu.
3. Click on Paste.

Clipboard—Saving Contents

You can save the text and graphics you copy or cut to the Clipboard as a specially formatted .CLP file you can open later in the Clipboard.

Keyboard Steps

1. After you've pasted text or graphics to the Clipboard, start the Clipboard Viewer.

2. Pull down the File menu .... **Alt** + **F**

3. Choose Save **A**s .... **A**

4. Choose the **D**irectory list .... **Alt** + **D**

5. Highlight and select the directory where you want to save the file .... **↑** or **↓**
   ↵

6. Move back to the File **N**ame box .... **Alt** + **N**

7. Type a name for the file of 8 characters or less .... ***filename***

*You could type **namelist** for a list of names you're saving, or **logo** for a graphic of your company logo.*

EXAMPLE

8. To finish, press .... **↵**

Mouse Steps

1. After you've pasted text or graphics to the Clipboard, start the Clipboard Viewer.

2. Click on the File menu.

Clipboard—Saving Contents

3. Click on Save **As**.

4. Double-click on the directory where you want to store the file in the **D**irectory list.

5. Type a name for the file of 8 characters or less in the File **N**ame box, as in *filename*.

6. To finish, click on **OK**.

Clipboard—Starting the Clipboard Viewer

You can view material you've cut or copied to the Clipboard, and save it to a Clipboard file, in the Clipboard Viewer.

Keyboard Steps

1. Highlight the Main program group from the Program Manager .... |Ctrl| + |Tab|

*You may have to press **Ctrl+Tab** several times to highlight the Main group icon.*

TIP

2. Press .... |↵|

3. Highlight the Clipboard Viewer icon .... |←|, |→|, |↑|, or |↓|

4. Press .... |↵|

Clipboard—Starting the Clipboard Viewer 13

Mouse Steps

1. At the Program Manager, double-click on Main program group icon.

2. In the Main program group window, double-click on Clipboard Viewer program-item icon.

Colors—Changing for a Screen Element

You can change the colors of any screen element you wish, such as window title bars, borders, and text.

TIP *Once you've changed several screen colors, you can save your changes as a color scheme. To do so, press **Alt+A** or click on the Save Scheme button. Type a name for the scheme in the dialog box that appears, then press **Enter** or click on **OK**.*

Keyboard Steps

1. Open the Color dialog box. (See "Colors— Opening the Color Dialog Box.")

2. Choose the Color **P**alette>> button .... Alt + P

3. Open the Screen **E**lement list .... Alt + E
   Alt + ↓

---

14   Clipboard—Starting the Clipboard Viewer

4. Select the screen element
   you want to change .... ↓ or ↑
   Tab

5. Select a color from the
   Basic Colors palette .... ↓, ↑, ←, or →
   Space

TIP *In steps 4 and 5, you may need to press the **arrow** keys or **Tab** key several times to highlight the selection you want.*

6. Repeat steps 3-5 to change the colors of other elements.

7. To close the Color dialog box, press .... ↵

Mouse Steps

1. Open the Color dialog box. (See "Colors—Opening the Color Dialog Box.")

2. Click on Color **P**alette>>.

3. In the sample screen at the left of the Color dialog box, click on the screen element you want to change.

Colors—Changing for a Screen Element

You can also use the Screen Element drop-down list to select which screen element to apply a color to.

4. In the Basic Colors area, click on the color you want.

You can create custom colors to assign to screen elements. Click on them in the Custom Colors area. See "Colors—Defining" to learn how.

5. Repeat steps 3-4 to change additional colors.
6. To close the Color dialog box, click on **OK**.

Colors—Choosing a New Scheme

Windows comes with several pre-defined color schemes you can select easily to jazz up your screen.

Keyboard Steps

1. Open the Color dialog box. (See "Colors—Opening the Color Dialog Box.")

2. Scroll through the list of Color **S**chemes, stopping at the one you prefer .... ↓ or ↑

3. When finished, press .... ↵

Colors—Changing for a Screen Element

Mouse Steps

1. Open the Color dialog box. (See "Colors—Opening the Color Dialog Box.")

2. At the right edge of the Color **S**chemes drop-down list, click on the down arrow.

3. To scroll through the list, click on and hold the scroll bar arrows.

4. Click on the scheme you want.

5. Click on **OK**.

Colors—Creating Custom

To make your desktop truly unique, Windows enables you to mix custom colors in the Color dialog box.

Don't forget to save your color scheme after you've mixed custom colors. See "Colors—Changing for a Screen Element."

Keyboard Steps

1. Open the Color dialog box. (See "Colors—Opening the Color Dialog Box.")

2. Choose the Color **P**alette>> button .... Alt + P

3. Choose **D**efine Custom Colors .... Alt + D

4. Choose one of the color mixing boxes:

   Hue .... `Alt` + `H`

   Sat (saturation) .... `Alt` + `S`

   Lum (luminosity) .... `Alt` + `L`

   Red .... `Alt` + `R`

   Green .... `Alt` + `G`

   Blue .... `Alt` + `B`

5. Type a value for the box .... **###**

EXAMPLE

You can enter 0 to 239 for Hue, 0 to 240 for Sat and Lum, and 0 to 255 for Red, Green, and Blue.

6. Repeat steps 4 and 5 as needed.

7. Choose the Add Color button .... `Alt` + `A`

8. Repeat steps 4-7 to create more colors.

9. When finished, press .... `↵`

Mouse Steps

1. Open the Color dialog box. (See "Colors—Opening the Color Dialog Box.")

2. Click on Color **P**alette>>.

3. Click on **D**efine Custom Colors.

4. In the color refiner box (sample color area), click on the color you want.

5. To adjust the luminosity, drag the arrow next to the vertical luminosity bar.

6. Click on **A**dd Color.

7. Repeat steps 4-6 to create more colors.

8. When finished, click on **C**lose.

Colors—Opening the Color Dialog Box

*To manipulate Windows screen colors, you must start by opening the **Color** dialog box from the Windows Control Panel.*

Keyboard Steps

1. Highlight the Main program group icon from the Program Manager .... `Ctrl` + `Tab`

2. Press .... `↵`

3. Highlight the Control Panel program-item icon .... `←`, `→`, `↑`, or `↓`

4. Press .... `↵`

5. Highlight the Color icon .... `←` or `→`

6. Press .... `↵`

Mouse Steps

1. At the Program Manager, double-click on the Main program group icon.

2. In the Main program group window, double-click on Control Panel program-item icon.

3. In the Control Panel window, double-click on the Color icon.

Desktop—Arranging

See "Icons—Arranging" and "Windows—Arranging."

Desktop—Customizing

*The Windows **desktop**—the background for the Program Manager—can be customized for your own preferences. Following are the options you can specify:*

Group	Options	Description
Pattern	Name	Chooses a pattern for the background
Applications	Fast "Alt+Tab" Switching	Lets you choose Alt+Tab to switch between applications
Screen Saver	Name	Lets you choose the name of a Windows screen saver
	Delay	Sets the amount of time with no typing or mouse movement before the screen saver displays

Colors—Opening the Color Dialog Box

	Test	Lets you preview the screen saver you've selected
	Setup	Choose this to set up the screen saver you've selected.
Wallpaper	File	Chooses a wallpaper picture to display on the desktop
	Center	Displays the wallpaper image in the center of the desktop
	Tile	Repeats the wallpaper image to fill the desktop
Icons	Spacing	Determines how close icons are placed when you choose Window Arrange Icons
	Wrap Title	Lets icon titles display in more than one line
Sizing Grid	Granularity	Specifying a value above 0 displays a grid on thedesktop
	Border Width	Sets a window border width
	Cursor Blink Rate	Specifies how often the cursor blinks

Desktop—Customizing

Keyboard Steps

1. Highlight the Main program group at the Program Manager ...... **Ctrl** + **Tab**

   *You may have to press **Ctrl+Tab** several times to highlight the Main group icon.*

   TIP

2. Press .... **↵**
3. Highlight the Control Panel icon .... **←**, **→**, **↑**, or **↓**
4. Press .... **↵**
5. Highlight the Desktop icon ... **←**, **→**, **↑**, or **↓**
6. Press .... **↵**
7. Specify the options you want .... **Alt** + *selectionletter* (if needed) .... *number* or *arrow keys*
8. Press .... **↵**

Mouse Steps

1. At the Program Manager, double-click on the Main program group icon.
2. Double-click on the Control Panel program-item icon.
3. Double-click on the Desktop icon.

Desktop—Customizing

4. To specify the options you want, click on the option **number** (or use the **arrow keys**).

5. Click on **OK**.

Directories—Creating

You can use the Windows File Manager to create new subdirectories on your hard disk or a floppy disk. A subdirectory is a named area on a disk designated to organize and store related files.

Keyboard Steps

1. Start the File Manager. (See "File Manager—Starting.")

2. Select a drive .... Ctrl + *drive*

EXAMPLE

*To select drive C:, press **Ctrl+C**; to select drive B:, press **Ctrl+B**; and so on.*

3. If you want to create a subdirectory of a directory other than the root, highlight another directory in the Directory Tree .... ↓ or ↑

TIP

*In step 3 you may need to press the **arrow** keys multiple times to highlight the directory you want.*

TIP *Press **Home** or \ (backslash) to move back to the root directory. Use **PageDown** and **PageUp** to move more quickly through the directories.*

4. Pull down the File menu .... **Alt** + **F**
5. Choose Create Directory .... **E**
6. Type a name (up to 8 characters) in the Name box .... ***name***

EXAMPLE *For example, you might type **smithco** to create a directory containing all the files pertaining to one of your clients.*

7. Press .... ⏎

Mouse Steps

1. Start the File Manager. (See "File Manager—Starting.")

2. To select a drive, click on the icon for the drive you want.

3. To scroll through the directories in the Directory Tree, click on and hold the scroll bar arrows.

4. To select a directory you want to make a subdirectory for, click on the directory name.

5. Click on the File menu.

Directories—Creating

6. Click on Create Directory.
7. Type a name up to 8 characters in the **Name** box, as in *name*.
8. Click on **OK**.

Directories—Viewing

When you select a directory in the Directory Tree at the left side of a File Manager directory window, the right side (File window) shows a list of the files that directory contains.

To view the contents of more than one directory simultaneously, you must open another directory window. See "Directory Window— Opening Additional."

Keyboard Steps

1. Start the File Manager. (See "File Manager—Starting.")
2. Select a drive .... **Ctrl** + *driveletter*

*To select drive C:, press **Ctrl+C**; to select drive B:, press **Ctrl+B**; and so on.*

3. Highlight the directory .... ↓ or ↑

4. If a directory contains a subdirectory you want to view, expand it .... `+`

5. Highlight the subdirectory you want to view .... `↓` or `↑`

Mouse Steps

1. Start the File Manager. (See "File Manager—Starting.")

2. To select a drive, click on the icon for the drive you want.

3. To scroll through the directories in the Directory Tree, click on and hold the scroll bar arrows.

4. To select a directory, click on the directory name.

5. To display subdirectories, double-click on the directory that contains them.

6. To view a subdirectory, click on its name.

Directory Tree—Expanding Levels

*By default, the Directory Tree is completely collapsed when you start File Manager. You can expand branches of the Directory Tree to view files, or even expand all the branches. (A **branch** is a directory with one or more levels of subdirectories.)*

*To collapse a branch you've selected, choose **Tree Collapse Branch** or press – (minus sign).*

Directories—Viewing

Keyboard Steps

1. Start the File Manager. (See "File Manager—Starting.")

2. Select a drive .... [Ctrl] + *driveletter*

EXAMPLE

*To select drive C:, press **Ctrl+C**; to select drive B:, press **Ctrl+B**; and so on.*

3. Highlight the directory .... [↓] or [↑]
4. Pull down the **T**ree menu .... [Alt] + [T]
5. Choose an expansion option:

   Ex**p**and One Level .... [X]
   Expand **B**ranch .... [B]
   Exp**a**nd All .... [A]

TIP

*Press the plus key (+) to expand one level and skip steps 4-5. Similarly, use the asterisk (*) to expand a branch, and **Ctrl+*** to expand all the branches.*

Mouse Steps

1. Start the File Manager. (See "File Manager—Starting.")

2. To select a drive, click on the icon for the drive you want.

Directory Tree—Expanding Levels

3. To scroll through the directories in the Directory Tree, click and hold the scroll bar arrows.

4. To select a directory, click on the directory name.

5. Click on the **Tree** menu.

6. Click on one of the following: E**x**pand One Level, Expand **B**ranch, Expand A**l**l.

Directory Tree—Selecting Drives and Directories

The Directory Tree for a disk drive appears in the left side of the directory window in the File Manager. Moving through the Directory Tree enables you to display and select files for many types of operations from the File list at the right.

*You may need to expand and collapse subdirectories as you move through the Directory Tree. See "Directory Tree—Expanding Levels." Use the **Tree I**ndicate Expandable Branches command to have Windows indicate expandable directories with a plus sign (+) in the directory icon.*

To select a floppy disk drive, you must place a diskette in the appropriate drive.

Directory Tree—Expanding Levels

Keyboard Instructions

1. Start the File Manager. (See "File Manager—Starting.")

2. Select a drive .... **Ctrl** + *driveletter*

EXAMPLE

*To select drive C:, press **Ctrl+C**; to select drive B:, press **Ctrl+B**; and so on.*

3. Highlight the directory .... ↓ or ↑

Mouse Steps

1. Start the File Manager. (See "File Manager—Starting.")

2. To select a drive, click on the icon for the drive you want.

3. To scroll through the directories in the Directory Tree, click on and hold the scroll bar arrows.

4. To select a directory, click on the directory name.

Directory Window—Arranging

When you have multiple directory windows open, you can maximize, minimize, tile, cascade, and drag them around as you would any other window. See "Windows—Arranging" for details about how to arrange windows.

Directory Window—Closing

Using the directory window's Control menu is the fastest way to close it. See "Windows—Closing" for details.

Directory Window—Moving the Split

Every directory window is split into two sides: the Directory Tree at left and the File list at right. A split bar (double line) to the left of the Directory Tree's scroll bar lets you adjust the width for each side of the directory window.

Keyboard Steps

1. Start the File Manager. (See "File Manager—Starting.")

2. Select the directory window you want to adjust .... **Ctrl** + **F6**

   *Press **Ctrl+F6** repeatedly until the window you want is active.*

3. Pull down the View menu .... **Alt** + **V**
4. Choose Split .... **L**

   *Press **Esc** to cancel the split operation.*

5. Reposition the vertical
   black split bar .... ← or →
6. Press .... ↵

Mouse Steps

1. Start the File Manager. (See "File Manager—Starting.")

2. To select the directory window you want to adjust, click on the directory window.

3. To display the split pointer, point to the split bar just to the right of the vertical scroll bar for the Directory Tree.

4. To move the split bar, drag the split pointer.

Directory Window—Opening Additional

To view different parts of the Directory Tree (or the files in more than one directory) simultaneously, open another directory window. Scrolling in one directory window will scroll the other; changes you make in one window will appear in the other when the same directories and files are visible.

Keyboard Steps

1. Start the File Manager. (See "File Manager—Starting.")

2. Pull down the **W**indow menu .... Alt + W

3. Choose **N**ew Window .... N

Mouse Steps

1. Start the File Manager. (See "File Manager—Starting.")
2. Double-click on a disk icon.

*If you double-click on the icon for a floppy drive and a dialog box tells you there's no disk in the drive, insert the disk and click on **Retry**.*

Directory Window— Refreshing the File List

*When you perform file operations (such as copying files) affecting a directory, the changes don't always show up in the File list. To update a directory's contents, you must **refresh** the directory window.*

Keyboard Steps

1. Select the directory window you want to adjust .... **Ctrl** + **F6**

*Press **Ctrl+F6** repeatedly until the window you want is active.*

2. Pull down the **W**indow menu .... **Alt** + **W**
3. Choose **R**efresh .... **R**

Directory Window—Opening Additional

Mouse Steps

1. To select the directory window to refresh, click on the directory window.
2. Click on the disk icon.

Disk—Copying

Through the File Manager, you can make a duplicate of any disk. Note that you must copy to a blank disk that's the same size (3 1/2 inches or 5 1/4 inches) and density (DD or HD) as the original disk. Unless your system is equipped with two identical floppy drives, you'll use only one drive to perform the copy procedure.

Keyboard Steps

1. Start the File Manager. (See "File Manager—Starting.")
2. Pull down the Disk menu .... [Alt] + [D]
3. Choose Copy Disk .... [C]

If you have only one disk drive on your system, skip to step 8.

4. Type the drive letter where you'll place the original disk (Source In) .... ***drive***

EXAMPLE *For example, type **b** for drive B:.*

5. Press .... `Tab`

6. Type the drive letter where you'll place the target, or copy to, disk (**Destination In**) .... ***drive***

Most users will make the copy using a single disk drive. Make sure you type the same drive letter in steps 4 and 6.

TIP

7. Press .... ⏎

8. To confirm the copy operation, press .... ⏎

9. Place the source (original disk) in the drive you specified. Press .... ⏎

10. Put in the target (copy) disk when Windows tells you to. Press .... ⏎

11. Repeat steps 9–10 as needed.

Disk—Copying

Mouse Steps

1. Start the File Manager. (See "File Manager—Starting.")
2. Click on the **D**isk menu.
3. Click on **C**opy Disk.

If you have only one disk drive on your system, skip to step 8.

4. Click on the down arrow, then the drive letter where you'll place the original disk (**S**ource In).

*For example, type **b** for drive B:.*

5. Click on **D**estination In.
6. Click on the drive letter where you'll place the target (or copy) disk.

Most users will make the copy using a single disk drive. Make sure you select the same drive letter in steps 4 and 6.

7. Click on **OK**.

Disk—Copying

8. To confirm the copy operation, click on **OK**.

9. Place the source (original disk) in the drive you specified. Click on **OK**.

10. Put in the target (copy) disk when Windows tells you to. Click on **OK**.

11. Repeat steps 9-10 as needed.

Disk—Formatting

Formatting prepares a diskette to store information. File Manager (and other Windows applications) can only read disks that have been formatted. If a disk isn't formatted, File Manager will ask if you want to format it.

Windows will not let you format your hard disk, because formatting a disk wipes out all the information on it. Formatting your hard drive would wipe out all your applications and data files—even Windows!

*Press **Esc** at any time to cancel a format operation.*

Keyboard Steps

1. Start the File Manager. (See "File Manager—Starting.")

2. Pull down the **D**isk menu .... `Alt` + `D`
3. Choose **F**ormat Disk .... `F`
4. Pull down the **D**isk In list .... `Alt` + `D`
   `Alt` + `↓`
5. Choose the floppy drive
   you'll use for formatting .... `↓` or `↑`

> **TIP** *Windows chooses the best Capacity automatically, on the basis of your Disk In selection. If this is the choice you want, skip steps 6 and 7.*

6. Pull down the **C**apacity list .... `Alt` + `C`
   `Alt` + `↓`
7. Select the capacity
   of the floppy disk
   you'll be formatting .... `↓` or `↑`
   `Tab`

> **TIP** *If you want, you can specify disk Options at this point. You can type in a Label to name the disk, copy the system files to the disk during formatting (**Make System Disk**), or quickly reformat a previously formatted disk (**Quick Format**).*

8. Press .... `↵`

Disk—Formatting

9. To continue formatting, press .... ⏎

10. When formatting is complete, choose whether or not to format another disk .... Y or N

Mouse Steps

1. Start the File Manager. (See "File Manager—Starting.")

2. Click on the **D**isk menu.

3. Click on Format Disk.

4. To pull down the **D**isk In list, click on its down arrow.

5. Click on the floppy drive you're using for formatting.

Windows chooses the best Capacity automatically, on the basis of your Disk In selection. If this is the choice you want, skip steps 6 and 7.

6. To pull down the **C**apacity list, click on its down arrow.

7. Click on the floppy disk capacity.

If you want, you can specify disk Options at this point. You can type in a Label to name the disk, copy the system files to the disk during formatting

Disk—Formatting

(Make System Disk), or quickly reformat a previously formatted disk (Quick Format).

8. Click on **OK**.
9. To continue formatting, click on **Yes**.
10. When formatting is complete, choose whether or not to format another disk. Click on **Yes** or **No**.

DOS Applications— Changing Settings

To control how a DOS application runs, without editing the Windows PIF (program information file), you can use the Settings option on the application's Control menu to change these settings "on the fly." Following is a summary of the available options.

Settings	Options	Description
Display Options	Window	Runs the application in a window
	Full Screen	Runs the application full-screen
Tasking Options (you can turn on both)	Exclusive	Stops other applications from running when the DOS application is active
	Background	Keeps the application running when it's in the background (not active)

continues

Settings	Options	Description
Priority	Foreground	Sets the application's running speed when it's active
	Background	Sets the application's running speed when it's not active (Tasking Options—Background must be selected, too)
Special	Terminate	Choose this only when you can't leave the application by normal means. CAUTION: THIS OPTION CAN RESULT IN LOST DATA. Restart your computer after using this button.

Keyboard Instructions

1. Go to the DOS application .... `Alt` + `Tab`

2. Pull down the application's Control menu .... `Alt` + `Space`

> *If Alt+Spacebar doesn't work, try Alt+Enter.*
>
> **TIP**

3. Choose Settings .... `T`

4. Choose a Display option:

   Window .... W

   or

   Full Screen .... U

5. Turn on one or both Tasking options:

   Exclusive X
   Background .... B

6. Move to the Foreground priority box .... F

7. Type a value of 1 to 10,000 .... ###

> **EXAMPLE**
> *For example, type **1000** to increase the speed or **25** to decrease it.*

8. Move to the Background priority box .... A

9. Type a value of 1 to 10,000 .... ###

10. Press .... ⏎

Mouse Steps

1. Click on the DOS application window, or double-click on the DOS application icon.

2. To pull down the application's Control menu, click on the Control menu box.

DOS Applications—Changing Settings 41

*If the application is running full-screen, you must press **Alt+Spacebar** to pull down its Control menu.*

3. Click on Settings.
4. Click on **W**indow or F**u**ll Screen.
5. Click on E**x**clusive and/or **B**ackground.
6. Highlight **F**oreground priority value.
7. Type a value of 1 to 10,000, as in **###**.

*For example, type **1000** to increase the speed or **25** to decrease it.*

8. Highlight **B**ackground priority value.
9. Type a value of 1 to 10,000, as in **###**.
10. Click on **OK**.

DOS Fonts—Changing

When you choose not to run a DOS application at full-screen size in Windows, you can choose a different font size to use in the window for the DOS application. The default font size is 8 x 8 pixels, but you can choose sizes from 4 x 6 to 16 x 12 pixels. Larger font sizes are particularly useful if your monitor has a very high resolution (which would tend to make the fonts look small).

If you change the font when the DOS application is running at full-screen size, Windows places the application in a window.

Keyboard Steps

1. Click on .... ***DOS application window***
2. Pull down the application Control menu .... `Alt` + `Space`
3. Choose Fonts .... `F`
4. Highlight the font you want in the Font list .... `↓` or `↑`
5. Press .... `↵`

Mouse Steps

1. Click on the DOS application window, or double-click on the DOS application icon.

2. To pull down the application's Control menu, click on the Control menu box.

*If the application is running full-screen, you must press **Alt+Spacebar** to pull down its Control menu.*

3. Click on Fonts.
4. Click on a font in the Font list.
5. Click on **OK**.

DOS Fonts—Changing

Drivers—Adding for Sound and Video

To run your video display (and any sound device you attach to your system), you must add a driver file to Windows that enables Windows to recognize the device. (You can add video drivers through Setup, and must use Setup to select the current video driver.) Some driver files are provided on your Windows disks; others come with the hardware when you purchase it.

TIP
*To set up a sound driver, select the **Drivers** icon from the Control Panel. Highlight your driver in the list of Installed Drivers, then choose the Setup button.*

Keyboard Instructions

1. Highlight the Main program group at the Program Manager ...... [Ctrl] + [Tab]

2. Press .... [↵]

3. Highlight the Control Panel program-item icon .... [←], [→], [↑], or [↓]

4. Press .... [↵]

5. Highlight the Drivers icon .... [←] or [→]

6. Choose **Add** .... [Alt] + [A]

7. Select the name of the
   driver you want to install
   in the List of drivers .... [↓] or [↑]
   [↵]

> **TIP** *If the driver you want isn't on the list, highlight **Unlisted or Updated driver**.*

8. Insert the driver disk when
   Windows asks for it. Press .... [↵]

> **TIP** *If the driver is already on your system, Windows asks whether you want to add a **N**ew driver or use the system's **C**urrent file.*

> **TIP** *Type in the appropriate disk drive letter if you need to, or use the **B**rowse button to find which directory contains the driver file.*

9. Press .... [↵]

10. In the Setup dialog box
    that appears, choose
    the appropriate settings:

    Speed .... [S]
    [←] or [→]

Drivers—Adding for Sound and Video   45

Volume .... **V**
⬅ or ➡

Limit .... **L**
⬅ or ➡

Enable interrupts
during playback .... **E**

11. Press .... ⏎

12. Choose **D**on't Restart Now
    or **R**estart Now .... **D** or **R**

Mouse Steps

1. At the Program Manager, double-click on the Main program group icon.

2. Double-click on the Control Panel program-item icon.

3. Double-click on the Drivers icon.

4. Click on **A**dd.

5. In the **L**ist of Drivers, double-click on the driver to install.

*If the driver you want isn't on the list, choose **Unlisted or Updated driver**.*

Drivers—Adding for Sound and Video

6. Insert the driver disk when Windows asks for it. Click on **OK**.

If the driver is already on your system, Windows asks whether you want to add a New driver or use the system's Current file.

*Type the appropriate disk drive letter if you need to, or use the **Browse** button to find which directory contains the driver file.*

7. Click on **OK**.

8. In the Setup dialog box that appears, click on the appropriate settings.

    Speed

    Volume

    Limit

    Enable interrupts during playback

9. Click on **OK**.

10. Click on **D**on't Restart Now or **R**estart Now.

Drivers—Adding for Sound and Video

Drivers—Selecting for Video

The Windows Setup facility lets you choose which of the installed video drivers the system should use.

Keyboard Instructions

1. Highlight the Main program group at the Program Manager ...... `Ctrl` + `Tab`

2. Press .... `↵`

3. Highlight the Windows Setup icon .... `←` or `→`

4. Press .... `↵`

5. Pull down the **O**ptions menu .... `Alt` + `O`

6. Choose **C**hange System Settings .... `C`

7. Pull down the **D**isplay list .... `D`

   `Alt` + `↓`

8. Select the driver from the list .... `↑` or `↓`

   `↵`

9. If Windows asks for a disk, insert it in the drive. Type a new driver letter (if needed), press .... `↵`
   or

specify Current or New for
a driver that's already
on your system .... R or N

10. Specify whether to Restart
Windows or Continue .... R or C

Mouse Steps

1. At the Program Manager, double-click on the Main program group icon.

2. Double-click on the Windows Setup program-item icon.

3. Click on the Options menu.

4. Click on Change System Settings.

5. To pull down the Display list, click on its down arrow.

6. Click on a driver from the list.

7. Click OK.

8. If Windows asks for a disk, insert it in the drive. Type a new driver letter (if needed), and click on OK (or, for a driver that's on your system, click on Current or New).

9. Click on either Restart Windows or Continue.

Drivers—Selecting for Video

File Manager—Options

You can change several File Manager options using the Options menu. Following is a summary of the option commands available.

In the following table, the commands that have no dialog box selections are toggles. Selecting one of these options turns it on or off. A check mark beside it means it's on.

Command	Dialog Box Selections	Effect When Selected
Confirmation	File Delete	Asks you to confirm file deletions
	Directory Delete	sks you to confirm Adirectory deletions
	File Replace	Asks you to confirm copy operations that replace an existing file
	Mouse Action	Asks you to confirm mouse file copy and move operations when dragging
	Disk Commands	Asks you to confirm disk formatting or copying
Font	Font	Chooses the font displayed in each directory window

	Font Style	Assigns a style to the font displayed in each directory window
	Size	Assigns a size to the font displayed in each directory window
	Lowercase	Makes the directory window text appear in lowercase letters
Status Bar	none	When checked, displays status bar at the bottom of the window
Minimize on use	none	When checked, reduces the File Manager to an icon when you start another application
Save Settings on **Exit**	none	When checked, saves the options you specified when you close File Manager

Keyboard Steps

1. Start the File Manager. (See "File Manager—Starting.")
2. Pull down the Options menu .... **Alt** + **O**

File Manager—Options 51

3. Choose an option .... ***selectionletter***

4. If a dialog box appears,
   make your choices .... `Alt` + ***selectionletter***
   `↑`, `↓` or `Space`

*In the preceding step, use **Alt+selectionletter** to select as many items as needed. Then use the arrow keys or **Spacebar** as needed to choose list or check box items.*

5. Press .... `⏎`

Mouse Steps

1. Start the File Manager. (See "File Manager—Starting.")
2. Click on the **O**ptions menu.
3. Click on the command.
4. Click on your dialog box choices.
5. Click on **OK**.

File Manager—Starting

File Manager is an application (program) that comes with Windows. It enables you to perform file, disk, and directory operations in a graphical environment.

Keyboard Steps

1. Highlight the Main program group at the Program Manager ...... `Ctrl` + `Tab`

*You may have to press **Ctrl+Tab** several times to highlight the Main group icon.*

2. Press .... ↵
3. Highlight the File
   Manager icon .... ←, →, ↑, or ↓
4. Press .... ↵

Mouse Steps

1. At the Program Manager, double-click on the Main program group icon.

2. Double-click on the File Manager program-item icon.

Files—Associating

*Windows File Manager lets you **associate** files. That is, you associate a file extension with an application; then, when you double-click on files with that extension (or highlight one of the files and press Enter), Windows starts the application and opens the selected file.*

For example, you might choose to associate all files that end in a .DOC extension with Word for DOS.

Keyboard Steps

1. Start the File Manager. (See "File Manager—Starting.")

2. Highlight the directory containing
   the file you want to associate .... [↓] or [↑]

3. Move to the File list .... [Tab]

4. Highlight the file
   to associate .... [←], [→], [↓], or [↑]

5. Pull down the File menu .... [Alt] + [F]

6. Choose Associate .... [A]

7. Move to the Associate With
   list box .... [Alt] + [A]
   [Tab]

8. Highlight the application
   to associate with the extension
   in the Files with Extension box .... [↓] or [↑]

You can use the Browse button to find applications that don't appear in the Associate With list.

TIP

9. Press .... [↵]

Mouse Steps

1. Start the File Manager. (See "File Manager—Starting.")

2. Click on the directory containing the file you want to associate.

3. In the File list, click on the file to associate.

Files—Associating

4. Click on the **File** menu.
5. Click on **Associate**.
6. Pull down the **Associate** With list box; click on its down arrow.
7. Click on the application to associate with the extension in the **Files** with Extension box.

To remove an association, choose (None) from the Associate With list.

8. Click on **OK**.

Files—Copying

In the File Manager, you can copy files from one drive and/or directory to another. If you're copying to a floppy disk in one drive from a floppy disk in another, be sure to place both disks in their respective drives.

If you try to copy a file to a disk and the disk already holds a file of that name, Windows asks you to confirm the copy operation.

Keyboard Steps

1. Start the File Manager. (See "File Manager—Starting.")

2. Place a disk in the disk drive to copy to.

3. Choose the drive to copy from .... **Ctrl** + *driveletter*

EXAMPLE

*To select drive C:, press **Ctrl+C**; to select drive B:, press **Ctrl+B**; and so on.*

4. Highlight the directory containing the file .... ↓ or ↑

5. Select the file(s) you want to copy (see "Files—Selecting").

6. Pull down the File menu .... **Alt** + **F**

7. Choose Copy .... **C**

TIP

*Pressing **F8** is a shortcut for steps 6 and 7.*

8. Type the drive to copy to, plus a colon .... *driveletter* :

TIP

*You can also type in a directory name to copy to a directory on the source disk. For example, typing **\temp** would copy the selected files to the \TEMP directory on the disk drive you selected in step 3.*

Files—Copying

9. Press ....

Mouse Steps

1. Start the File Manager. (See "File Manager—Starting.")

2. Place a disk in the disk drive to copy to (or from).

3. To select the drive to copy from, click on the icon for the drive you want.

4. To scroll through the directories in the Directory Tree, click and hold the scroll bar arrows.

5. To select a directory, click on the directory name.

6. Select the file(s) you want to copy (see "Files—Selecting").

7. Drag the highlighted files to the icon for the drive (or directory) to copy to. (NOTE: Hold down the **Ctrl** key while dragging if you're copying from one directory to another on the same disk.)

8. After releasing the mouse button, click on **OK**.

TIP

If the icon for the directory you want to copy to isn't visible, open a second directory window and scroll to it. See "Directory Window—Opening Additional."

Files—Copying

Files—Deleting

In the File Manager, you can delete files you no longer need from any drive or directory. If you want to delete all the files in a directory, you can use these steps, as well.

Keyboard Steps

1. Start the File Manager. (See "File Manager—Starting.")

2. If needed, place the disk with the file you want to delete in the disk drive.

3. Select the drive .... **Ctrl** + *driveletter*

EXAMPLE

*To select drive C:, press **Ctrl+C**; to select drive B:, press **Ctrl+B**; and so on.*

4. Highlight the directory holding the file .... ↓ or ↑

5. Select the file(s) you want to delete (see "Files—Selecting").

6. Pull down the File menu .... **Alt** + **F**

7. Choose Delete .... **D**

TIP

*Pressing **Delete** is a shortcut for steps 6 and 7.*

8. To continue the delete operation, press ......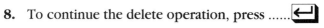

9. To confirm the deletion(s), press ....

Yes to All lets you confirm the deletion of multiple files. You can turn delete confirmation off using the Options Confirmation File Manager command.

Mouse Steps

1. Start the File Manager. (See "File Manager —Starting.")

2. If needed, place the disk holding the file to delete in the disk drive.

3. To select the drive, click on the icon for the drive you want.

4. To scroll through the directories in the Directory Tree, click on and hold the scroll bar arrows.

5. To select a directory, click on the directory name.

6. Select the file(s) you want to delete (see "Files— Selecting").

7. Click on the **File** menu.

8. Click on **Delete**.

9. To continue the delete operation, click on **OK**.

10. To confirm the deletion, click on **Yes** or Yes to All.

Files—Deleting

Files—Moving

File Manager enables you to move a file from one disk or directory to another.

Keyboard Steps

1. Start the File Manager. (See "File Manager—Starting.")

2. Place a disk in the disk drive to move files to.

3. Select the drive to move files from .... **Ctrl** + *driveletter*

EXAMPLE

*To select drive C:, press **Ctrl+C**; to select drive B:, press **Ctrl+B**; and so on.*

4. Highlight the directory holding the file .... ↓ or ↑

5. Select the file(s) you want to move (see "Files—Selecting").

6. Pull down the File menu .... **Alt** + **F**

7. Choose Move .... **M**

TIP

*Pressing **F7** is a shortcut for steps 6 and 7.*

8. Type the drive to move **T**o,
   plus a colon .... ***driveletter***
   :

*You can also type in a directory name to copy to a directory on the source disk. For example, typing **temp** would copy the selected files to the \TEMP directory on the disk drive you selected in step 3.*

9. Press .... ⏎

10. If you need to confirm a
    file replacement, press .... ⏎

Mouse Steps

1. Start the File Manager. (See "File Manager —Starting.")

2. Place a disk in the disk drive to move files to (or from).

3. To select the drive to move files from, click on the icon for the drive you want.

4. To scroll through the directories in the Directory Tree, click on and hold the scroll bar arrows.

5. To select a directory, click on the directory name.

6. Select the file(s) you want to move (see "Files—Selecting").

7. Press and hold Shift.

Files—Moving

8. Drag the highlighted files to the icon for the drive (or directory) to move files to.

9. After releasing the mouse button, click on **OK**.

TIP

If the icon for the directory you want to move to isn't visible, open a second directory window and scroll to it. See "Directory Window—Opening Additional."

Files—Renaming

Use the File Manager to give a new name for any file.

TIP

You can use these steps to rename directories.

Keyboard Steps

1. Start the File Manager. (See "File Manager—Starting.")

2. Place the disk holding the file to rename in the disk drive.

3. Select the drive holding the file .... **Ctrl** + *driveletter*

EXAMPLE

*To select drive C:, press **Ctrl+C**; to select drive B:, press **Ctrl+B**; and so on.*

Files—Moving

4. Highlight the directory
   holding the file .... ⬇ or ⬆

5. Select the file (or files) you
   want to rename. (See
   "Files—Selecting.")

6. Pull down the File menu .... Alt + F

7. Choose Rename .... N

8. In the To box, type the new
   file name .... *filename.ext*

You can also type in a directory name to move the file to a directory on the source disk. For example, typing \temp would move the selected file to the \TEMP directory on the disk drive you selected in step 3.

You can use wild-card characters to rename multiple files. The asterisk (*) can stand for a group of characters, while the question mark (?) can stand for a single character. For example, if you selected several files in step 5 and you want to rename all of them with the DOC extension, you would type *.DOC in this step.

9. Press .... ⏎

Mouse Steps

1. Start the File Manager. (See "File Manager—Starting.")

Files—Renaming

2. Place the disk holding the file to rename in the disk drive.

3. To select the drive holding the file, click on the icon for the drive.

4. To scroll through the directories in the Directory Tree, click on and hold the scroll bar arrows.

5. To select a directory, click on the directory name.

6. Select the file you want to rename (see "Files—Selecting").

7. Click on the File menu.

8. Click on Rename.

9. In the To box, type the new file name, as in *filename.ext*.

TIP

You can also type in a directory name to move the file to a directory on the source disk. For example, typing \temp would move the selected file to the \TEMP directory on the disk drive you selected in step 3.

TIP

You can use wild-card characters to rename multiple files. The asterisk (*) can stand for a group of characters, while the question mark (?) can stand for a single character. For example, if you selected several files in step 6 and you wanted to rename all of them with the DOC extension, you would type *.DOC in this step.

Files—Renaming

10. Click on **OK**.

Files—Running

Just as you can start applications from the Program Manager, the File Manager lets you start any executable (application) file. You can also open a file for which you've created an association (see "Files—Association"), starting the application in which it was created.

TIP

Executable files have the following extensions: .BAT, .COM, .EXE, and .PIF.

Keyboard Steps

1. Start the File Manager. (See "File Manager—Starting.")

2. Place the disk holding the file to start in the disk drive.

3. Select the drive holding the file .... **Ctrl** + *driveletter*

EXAMPLE

*To select drive C:, press **Ctrl+C**; to select drive B:, press **Ctrl+B**; and so on.*

4. Highlight the directory holding the file .... ↓ or ↑

Files—Running 65

5. Select the file you want to run. (See "Files—Selecting.")

6. Pull down the File menu .... Alt + F

7. Choose Run .... R

8. Press .... ↵

Mouse Steps

1. Start the File Manager. (See "File Manager—Starting.")

2. Place the disk holding the file to run in the disk drive.

3. To select the drive holding the file, click on the icon for the drive.

4. To scroll through the directories in the Directory Tree, click on and hold the scroll bar arrows.

5. To select a directory, click on the directory name.

6. Select the file you want to run. (See "Files—Selecting.")

7. Click on the File menu.

8. Click on Run.

9. Click on OK.

Double-clicking on the name of an executable file also starts it. If the file is not an executable file, but you've used File Manager to associate it with an

application, double-clicking on the file will start the application it's associated with—and open the file.

Files—Searching for

*Use the File Manager to find a file when you don't remember where it's stored or what it's named. Use **wildcards**, described below, to aid in your search.*

Wild-card Character	Use to	Example
*	Stand for any group of characters	*.BAK stands for all files with the .BAK extension.
?	Stand for any single character	FILE?.* stands for any file that begins with "FILE" and has one more character.

Keyboard Steps

1. Start the File Manager. (See "File Manager—Starting.")

2. Place the disk holding the file(s) to search for in the disk drive.

3. Pull down the File menu .... `Alt` + `F`

4. Choose Search .... `H`

5. Type the file name (or wild-cards) to Search For .... *filename.ext*

6. Press .... Tab

7. Type the disk and directory
   name to Start From .... *c:\directory*

8. Select or deselect the Search All
   Subdirectories check box .... Alt + E

9. Press .... ⏎

Mouse Steps

1. Start the File Manager. (See "File Manager—Starting.")

2. Place the disk holding the file(s) to search for in the disk drive.

3. Click on the File menu.

4. Click on Search.

5. Type the file name (or wildcards) to Search For, as in *filename.ext*.

6. Double-click on the Start From box.

7. Type the disk and directory name to start from, as in *c:\directory*.

8. To specify whether or not to search all subdirectories, click on the Search All Subdirectories check box.

9. Click on **OK**.

Files—Selecting

*Before you can perform many File Manager operations, you must **select** (highlight) one or more files. Note that you can also use the File Select Files command and type in a name or wild-card indicator of the file(s) to select.*

Keyboard Steps

1. Start the File Manager (See "File Manager—Starting.")

2. Select a drive .... Ctrl + *driveletter*

EXAMPLE

*To select drive C:, press **Ctrl+C**; to select drive B:, press **Ctrl+B**; and so on.*

3. Highlight the directory you want .... ↓ or ↑

TIP

*At this point, you could press **Ctrl+/** (slash) to select all files in the highlighted directory.*

4. To move to the file list, press .... Tab
5. Highlight the file you want .... ←, →, ↓, or ↑

TIP

*To select additional files adjacent to the one that's already selected, press **Shift+↓** or **Shift+↑**. To select additional files that aren't in sequence, press **Shift+F8**, highlight each additional file you want and press **Spacebar**, then press **Shift+F8** again.*

Mouse Steps

1. Start the File Manager (See "File Manager—Starting.")

2. To select a drive, click on the icon for the drive you want.

3. To scroll through the directories in the Directory Tree, click on and hold the scroll bar arrows.

4. To select a directory, click on the directory name.

5. To select the file, click on the file name in the file list.

TIP

*To select multiple contiguous files with the mouse, click on the first file, hold down **Shift**, and click on the second file. To select several unattached files, hold down **Ctrl**, then click on each file you want.*

Files—Viewing

Sometimes you may want to see only certain kinds of files in the selected directory. Or, you might want to see more details about the files stored there. The

File Manager View menu provides numerous options for how the files in the file list are displayed and sorted, as follows:

Command	Dialog Box Selections	Effect When Selected
Tree and Directory	none	Displays the Directory Tree and the file list in the directory window
Tree Only	none	Displays the Directory Tree only in the directory window
Directory Only	none	Displays the file list only in the directory window
Split	See "Directory Window—Moving the Split"	
Name	none	Displays file names only in the file list
All File Details	none	Displays all de-tails about the file in the file list (see the selections listed next under **P**artial File Details)
Partial File Details **S**ize		Displays the size of the file (in bytes) in the file list

continues

Files—Viewing

Command	Dialog Box Selections	Effect When Selected
	Last Modification Date	Displays the system date when you last saved the file
	Last Modification Time	Displays the system time when you last saved the file
	File Attributes	Displays any attributes you assign with the File Properties command
Sort by Name	none	Sorts files in the file list alphabetically by name
Sort by Type	none	Sorts files in the file list alphabetically by extension
Sort by Size	none	Sorts files in the file list by size in bytes, from the largest down
Sort by Date	none	Sorts files in the file list by last modification date, from most recent back

By File Type	Name	Lets you enter a file name to display, or wildcards to display certain files only
	Directories	Displays directories in the file list
	Programs	Displays executable (program) files in the file list
	Documents	Displays document (text and graphics) files in the file list
	Other Files	Displays files of other types (such as program configuration files) in the file list
	Show Hidden/System Files	Displays files that would otherwise be hidden to prevent deletion in the file list

*In the preceding table, the commands that have no dialog box selections are **toggles**. Selecting one of these options turns it on or off. A check mark beside it means it's on.*

Files—Viewing 73

The settings you select using the View menu affect only the currently selected directory window. See "Windows— Selecting" to learn how to select a directory window in the File Manager.

Keyboard Steps

1. Start the File Manager. (See "File Manager—Starting.")
2. Pull down the View menu .... **Alt** + **V**
3. Select an option .... *selectionletter*
4. If a dialog box appears, make your choices .... **Alt** + *selectionletter*

   or

   selectionletter
   (in the By File Type Name box, type a file name or wild-card characters)

In the preceding step, use Alt+selectionletter or selectionletter to select as many items as needed.

5. Press .... ↵

Files—Viewing

Mouse Steps

1. Start the File Manager. (See "File Manager—Starting.")
2. Click on the View menu.
3. Click on a command.
4. Click on Your dialog box choices (in the By File Type Name box, type a file name or wild-card characters).
5. Click on **OK**.

Fonts—Adding

To use additional fonts with your Windows applications, you must add (install) the fonts to Windows using the Control Panel. Adding a font automatically causes it to appear in font lists for Windows applications.

Keyboard Instructions

1. Highlight the Main program group at the Program Manager ...... Ctrl + Tab

*You may have to press **Ctrl+Tab** several times to highlight the Main group icon.*

TIP

2. Press .... ⏎
3. Highlight the Control Panel icon .... ←, →, ↑, or ↓

4. Press .... ⏎

5. Highlight the Fonts icon .... ←, →, ↑, or ↓

6. Press .... ⏎

7. Choose Add .... Alt + A

8. Select the drive to install from .... Alt + V
                                              ↑ or ↓
                                                 ⏎

EXAMPLE

*To select drive A:, you would press **Alt+A**, use the ↑ and ↓ keys to highlight **a:**, then press **Enter**.*

9. Select the directory to install from ..... Alt + D
                                               ↑ or ↓
                                                ⏎

10. Select the font(s) to install from
    the list .... Alt + F
                                            Shift + F8
                                              ↑ or ↓
                                                 Space
                                            Shift + F8

TIP

*Use the **arrow** keys plus the **Spacebar** repeatedly in the preceding step to select as many fonts as you wish to install.*

Fonts—Adding

*Make sure the Copy Fonts to Windows Directory check box is selected, unless you wish to install the font in a directory that's separate from the rest of your Windows fonts. Press **Alt+C** if you need to select it.*

11. Press .... ⏎

Mouse Steps

1. At the Program Manager, double-click on the Main program group icon.

2. Double-click on the Control Panel program-item icon.

3. Double-click on the Fonts icon.

4. Click on **A**dd.

5. Click on the down arrow beside the Dri**v**e list.

6. Click on the drive that holds the font(s) to install.

7. To select the directory to install from, double-click on it in the **D**irectory list.

8. To select the font to install, click on its name in the **F**onts list.

*Hold **Shift** and click to select multiple contiguous files. Hold **Ctrl** and click to select individual files.*

Fonts—Adding

*Make sure the Copy Fonts to Windows Directory check box is selected, unless you wish to install the font in a directory that's separate from the rest of your Windows fonts. Press **Alt+C** if you need to select it.*

9. Click on **OK**.

Fonts—Removing

Having many fonts gives you a lot of options to produce attractive formatting in your Windows applications. However, the fonts use precious memory when you're running Windows. You can recapture this memory by removing the fonts you rarely use from the list of fonts available to Windows.

Keyboard Instructions

1. Highlight the Main program group at the Program Manager ...... [Ctrl] + [Tab]

*You may have to press **Ctrl+Tab** several times to highlight the Main group icon.*

2. Press .... [↵]
3. Highlight the Control Panel icon .... [←], [→], [↑], or [↓]
4. Press .... [↵]
5. Highlight the Fonts icon .... [←], [→], [↑], or [↓]

6. Press .... ⏎

7. Select the font(s) to remove
   from the list .... Alt + F
   Shift + F8
   ↑ or ↓
   Space
   Shift + F8

*Use the **arrow** keys plus the **Spacebar** repeatedly in the preceding step to select as many fonts as you wish to remove.*

8. Press .... ⏎

Mouse Steps

1. At the Program Manager, double-click on the Main program group icon.

2. Double-click on the Control Panel program-item icon.

3. Double-click on the Fonts icon.

4. To select the font to install, click on its name in the Fonts list.

*Hold **Shift** and click to select multiple contiguous files. Hold **Ctrl** and click to select individual files.*

Fonts—Removing

5. Click on **OK**.

Hardware Settings

*If you change one of the basic components attached to your system (**Display**, **Keyboard**, **Mouse**, or **Network**), you'll need to let Windows know which device it is currently working with, using the Windows Setup program in the Main program group.*

*Windows most likely will ask you for a disk with a **driver file** for the new piece of hardware. If the driver is on a Windows disk, Windows will ask for that disk. If the driver is on a disk that came with your hardware, insert that disk when prompted.*

Keyboard Steps

1. Highlight the Main program group at the Program Manager ...... Ctrl + Tab

*You may have to press **Ctrl+Tab** several times to highlight the Main group icon.*

2. Press .... ⏎
3. Highlight the Windows Setup icon .... ←, →, ↑, or ↓
4. Press .... ⏎
5. Choose the Options menu .... Alt + O

Fonts—Removing

6. Choose **C**hange System Settings .... `C`

7. Pull down the list for
   the hardware item .... `Alt` + *selectionletter*
   `↓`

8. Highlight the name of
   your hardware .... `↓` or `↑`

9. Press .... `↵`

10. When Windows asks for it, insert a
    disk in drive A:, and press .... `↵`
    or
    Confirm that Windows can use the
    driver file found on your system, ... `R`
    or
    Tell Windows to use a **N**ew driver file, ... `N`
    insert the disk, and press .... `↵`

11. So that your changes will take
    effect, choose **R**estart Windows .... `R`

Mouse Steps

1. At the Program Manager, double-click on the Main program group icon.

2. Double-click on the Windows Setup program-item icon.

3. Click on the **O**ptions menu.

4. Click on **C**hange System Settings.

5. To pull down the list for the hardware item, click on its down arrow.

Hardware Settings

6. Click on the name of your hardware.
7. Click on **OK**.
8. When Windows asks for it, insert a disk in drive A:, and click on **OK**.
   or
   Confirm that Windows can use the driver file found on your system; click on Current.
   or
   Tell Windows to use a **N**ew driver file; click on New, then: Insert the disk. Click on **OK**.
9. So that your changes will take effect, click on **R**estart Windows.

Help

*Windows offers **context-sensitive** help—you get advice based on what you're currently doing in Windows when you display Help. When you display the Help screen, there are many options for getting more information or working with the information that's there. Help offers several menus with commands, and several buttons you can choose to move around.*

Menu	Command	Description
File	**O**pen	Lets you open specific Windows Help files
	Print Topic	Prints the text in the active Help window
	Print Setup	Lets you change printer settings

Hardware Settings

	Exit	Closes Help
Edit	Copy	Copies the text in the active Help window to the Clipboard
	Annotate	Lets you add your own notes to any Help screen
Bookmark	Define	Lets you specify places in help you can quickly jump to
	number	Selects the number of the bookmark you want to jump to
Help		Has commands which help you navigate

TIP

*Choose commands in the Help system just as you would elsewhere in Windows. Press **Alt+selection letter** or click to pull down a menu. Then press the **selection letter**, or click on the command you want.*

Button	**Description**
Contents	Returns you to the Help Contents screen
Search	Displays a dialog box so you can enter a topic to search for

continues

Button	Description
Back	Returns you to the previous Help screen
History	Lists the Help topics you've viewed during the current Help session, so you can select one and return to it
Glossary	Displays a list of terms you can select to get a definition for

*Click on a button to choose it, or press **Alt+selection letter**.*

TIP

To start off in Help, use the following steps.

Keyboard Steps

1. Pull down the Help menu .... `Alt` + `H`
2. Choose **C**ontents .... `C`
3. Move to the first highlighted, underlined topic .... `Tab`
4. Highlight the topic you want to see .... `↓` or `↑`
5. Press .... `↵`

Mouse Steps

1. Click on the **H**elp menu.
2. Click on **C**ontents.
3. Click on the topic you want to see.

Icons—Arranging

Windows can arrange the icons automatically in a window for you.

*An **icon** is a picture that represents a program or file.*

Keyboard Steps

1. Select the window with
   the icons to arrange .... Ctrl + F6
2. Pull down the **W**indow menu .... Alt + W
3. Choose Arrange Icons .... A

Mouse Steps

1. To select the window to arrange, click on the window.
2. Click on the **W**indow menu.
3. Click on **A**rrange Icons.

You can drag any icon to a new position.

Icons—Selecting

You need to select icons in the Program Manager before you can move or copy them.

Keyboard Steps—Program Group Icons

1. Go to the Program Manager.
2. Pull down the Window menu .... **Alt** + **W**
3. Choose the group's number .... ***number***

EXAMPLE

If you want the Accessories group, and it has a 2 beside it on the menu, press 2.

Keyboard Steps—Program Item Icons

1. Go to the Program Manager.
2. Choose the correct program group as just described.
3. Highlight the icon .... **→**, **←**, **↑**, or **↓**

Mouse Steps—Program Group Icons

1. Go to the Program Manager.
2. Click on the Program Group icon.

Double-click on any Program Group icon to open it.

Mouse Steps—Program Item Icons

1. Go to the Program Manager.
2. Double-click on the Program Group icon.
3. Click on the Program Item icon.

International Options

To customize Windows to work with the rules for another country (language), use the Control Panel. When you open the International icon, a dialog box appears with the following options.

Option	Description
Country	Selects all the standard settings (currency, date, etc.) for a country
Language	Chooses the language to work in for correct sorting
Keyboard Layout	Changes the characters keys represent to accommodate special characters
Measurement	Lets you choose a system of measurement

continues

Option	Description
List Separator	Lets you type in the character you want to separate lists of items
Date Format	Lets you specify how dates are displayed in applications
Time Format	Lets you specify how times are displayed in applications
Currency Format	Lets you choose the default for how currency is displayed
Number Format	Lets you choose default number display for applications

Keyboard Steps

1. Highlight the Main program group at the Program Manager ...... `Ctrl` + `Tab`

*You may have to press **Ctrl+Tab** several times to highlight the Main group icon.*

2. Press .... `↵`

3. Highlight the Control Panel icon .... `←`, `→`, `↑`, or `↓`

4. Press .... `↵`

5. Highlight the International icon .... `←`, `→`, `↑`, or `↓`

6. Press .... `↵`

International Options

7. Specify the **C**ountry, **L**anguage, **K**eyboard Layout, and **M**easurement options as needed .... `Alt` + *selectionletter* `↓` or `↑`

8. Enter a new List **S**eparator .... `Alt` + `S` *character*

9. Specify **D**ate Format, **T**ime Format, **Cu**rrency Format, and **N**umber Format changes as needed .... `Alt` + *selectionletter*
Fill in the dialog box.
Press .... `↵`

10. Press .... `↵`

Mouse Steps

1. At the Program Manager, double-click on the Main program group icon.

2. Double-click on the Control Panel program-item icon.

3. Double-click on the International icon.

4. Specify the **C**ountry, **L**anguage, **K**eyboard Layout, and **M**easurement options as needed. Click on the down arrow beside any list, then click on your choice.

International Options 89

5. Enter a new List Separator. Click in the box. Type a ***character***, such as **:**.

6. Specify **D**ate Format, **T**ime Format, **Cu**rrency Format, and **N**umber Format changes as needed. Click on the **Change** button for the option, fill in the dialog box, then click on **OK**.

7. Click on **OK**.

Keyboard—Modifying

You can modify the rate (speed) at which the cursor moves on-screen, and the rate at which Windows interprets each keystroke. Delay Before First Repeat is the length of time Windows waits before it repeats the keystroke when you hold the key down. Repeat Rate is how fast a key repeats when you hold it down.

Keyboard Steps

1. Highlight the Main program group at the Program Manager ...... **Ctrl** + **Tab**

*You may have to press **Ctrl+Tab** several times to highlight the Main group icon.*

TIP

2. Press .... **↵**

3. Highlight the Control Panel icon .... **←**, **→**, **↑**, or **↓**

4. Press .... **↵**

5. Highlight the Keyboard
   icon .... ←, →, ↑, or ↓
6. Press .... ↵
7. Choose **D**elay Before First Repeat ...... Alt + D
8. Slide the scroll box .... ← or →
9. Choose **R**epeat Rate .... Alt + R
10. Slide the scroll box .... ← or →
11. (Optional) Choose **T**est .... Alt + T
12. Type .... ***test text***
13. Repeat steps 7–12 as needed.
14. Press .... ↵

Mouse Steps

1. At the Program Manager, double-click on the Main program group icon.
2. Double-click on the Control Panel program-item icon.
3. Double-click on the Keyboard icon.
4. Drag the **D**elay Before First Repeat scroll box.
5. Drag the **R**epeat Rate scroll box.
6. To test settings, click in the **T**est text box.
7. Type some ***test text***.
8. Repeat steps 4–7 as needed.
9. Click on **OK**.

Keyboard—Modifying

Links—Creating

*Some Windows applications support Object Linking and Embedding (OLE), which means you can take information (an **object**) created in one document and place it in another. When you **link** an object into a client document, you create a reference to the original object in the source document. Updating the object in the client document also updates it in the source document. For more on embedding, see "Objects—Embedding."*

Keyboard Steps

1. Start the application and open the source document.

2. Select the object you want to link.

3. Pull down the Edit menu .... **Alt** + **E**

4. Choose Copy .... **C**

5. Go to the application you want to link to.

6. Open the client document that will accept the linked object; position the cursor.

7. Pull down the Edit menu .... **Alt** + **E**

8. Choose Paste Link .... **L**

TIP *Choose the Paste Special command to specify another **D**ata Type for the linked object. Then use the Paste Link button to finish the link.*

Mouse Steps

1. Start the application and open the source document.
2. Select the object you want to link.
3. Click on the **E**dit menu.
4. Click on **C**opy.
5. Go to the application you want to link to.
6. Open the client document that will accept the linked object; position the cursor.
7. Click on the **E**dit menu.
8. Click on Paste **L**ink.

TIP *Choose the Paste Special command to specify another Data Type for the linked object. Then use the Paste Link button to finish the link.*

Links—Updating

You can control several aspects of a link—like whether the object is updated automatically or manually—and edit the linked object using the Links dialog box. Following are the options available.

TIP *The options described in the following list may be different from those offered in the application you're working with. Consult the documentation for your application if you need additional information about how it updates links.*

Option	Description
Automatic	Updates the linked object every time the object is edited in the source application
Manual	Only updates the linked object when you choose Update Now
Locked	Prevents link updates
Open Source	Starts the source application so you can edit and save the object
Update Now	Updates the linked object when you have updating set to Manual
Cancel Link	Breaks the link between the object and the source application, leaving a copy of the object in the document
Change Link	Lets you change the source object to which the client object is linked

Keyboard Steps

1. Start the client application and document.
2. Select the linked object.
3. Pull down the Edit menu .... **Alt** + **E**
4. Choose Links .... **L**
5. Select one of the options .... **Alt** + *selectionletter*

*For example, press **Alt+U** to choose Update Now.*

EXAMPLE

TIP *If you chose Open Source, edit and save the file. If you chose Change Link, make the necessary edits and press Enter.*

6. Press .... ⏎

Mouse Steps

1. Start the client application and document.
2. Select the linked object.
3. Click on the Edit menu.
4. Click on Links.
5. Click on an option.

TIP *If you chose Open Source, edit and save the file. If you chose Change Link, make the necessary edits and press Enter.*

6. Click on **OK**.

Mode—386 Enhanced Options

*When you run more than one application when Windows is in 386 Enhanced mode, you may need to determine how certain resources—COM ports and the processor—are shared. To do so, you choose the **386 Enhanced** icon in Control Panel. This gives you the following settings:*

Setting	Options	Description
Device Contention		Choose which COM port to change the options for.
	Always Warn	Warns you if an application tries to use a port that's being used
	Never Warn	Lets any application use any port any time; NOT RECOMMENDED
	Idle	Enter a time for which a port must be idle before an application can use it.
Scheduling	Windows in Foreground	Enter a value to set how much processor time Windows applications can have when a Windows application is active.
	Windows in Background	Enter a value to set how much processor time Windows applications can have when a DOS application is active.

	Exclusive in Foreground	Suspends DOS applications in the background when a Windows application is active
Minimum Timeslice		Sets the minimum processor time given to an application before switching (*timeslice*). All Windows applications share the same timeslice.
Virtual Memory	Change	Displays a dialog box that lets you change how the Windows *swap-file* (memory created on your hard disk) is set up

Keyboard Steps

1. Highlight the Main program group at the Program Manager ...... `Ctrl` + `Tab`

2. Press .... `↵`

3. Highlight the Control Panel program-item icon .... `←`, `→`, `↑`, or `↓`

4. Press .... `↵`

5. Highlight the 386 Enhanced icon .... `←`, `→`, `↑`, or `↓`

Mode—386 Enhanced Options

6. Press .... ⏎

7. Specify options .... **Alt** + *selectionletter*
   (if needed, type in) .... *number*

8. Press .... ⏎

Mouse Steps

1. At the Program Manager, double-click on the Main program group icon.

2. In the Main program group window, double-click on the Control Panel program-item icon.

3. In the Control Panel window, double-click on the 386-Enhanced icon.

4. Click on the option to change (if necessary, enter a *number* into the appropriate text box).

5. Click on **OK**.

Mouse—Customizing

You can customize how your mouse works in Windows. Mouse Tracking Speed sets how fast the pointer moves. Double Click Speed affects how slow a double-click Windows can recognize. Swap Left/Right Buttons determines which is the primary mouse button. Mouse Trails displays the path of the mouse, using several icons.

The mouse you have with your system determines which options you have available in this dialog box. You may have more or fewer options than described here. See your mouse documentation.

Keyboard Steps

1. Highlight the Main program group at the Program Manager ...... [Ctrl] + [Tab]

*You may have to press **Ctrl+Tab** several times to highlight the Main group icon.*

2. Press .... [↵]
3. Highlight the Control Panel icon .... [←], [→], [↑], or [↓]
4. Press .... [↵]
5. Highlight the Mouse icon ...... [←], [→], [↑], or [↓]
6. Press .... [↵]
7. Choose **M**ouse Tracking Speed .... [Alt] + [M]
8. Slide the scroll box .... [←] or [→]
9. Choose **D**ouble Clicking Speed .... [Alt] + [D]
10. Slide the scroll box .... [←] or [→]
11. (Optional) Choose **S**wap Left/Right Buttons .... [Alt] + [S]
12. (Optional) Choose Mouse **T**rails .... [Alt] + [T]
13. Press .... [↵]

Mouse Steps

1. At the Program Manager, double-click on the Main program group icon.

Mouse—Customizing 99

2. Double-click on the Control Panel program-item icon.

3. Double-click on the Mouse icon.

4. Drag the **M**ouse Tracking Speed scroll box.

5. Drag the **D**ouble Click Speed scroll box.

6. To test settings, double-click in the **TEST** box.

7. Click on the **S**wap Left/Right Buttons.

8. Click on the Mouse **T**rails check box.

9. Click on **OK**.

Objects—Embedding

*Some Windows applications support **Object Linking and Embedding** (OLE), which means you can take information (an object) created in one document and place it in another. When you **embed** an object into a client document, you create a copy of the original object in the source document. You can select the object and open the source application to update the client document. This does not update it in the source document. For more on linking, see "Links—Creating."*

*Some applications let you insert an original embedded object (one not copied from a source application, but created by opening the source application from the client document) with **I**nsert Object, **E**dit Insert New Object, or a similar command.*

Keyboard Steps

1. Start the application and open the source document.
2. Select the object you want to link.
3. Pull down the Edit menu .... [Alt] + [E]
4. Choose Copy .... [C]
5. Go to the application you want to link to.
6. Open the client document that will accept the linked object; position the cursor.
7. Pull down the Edit menu .... [Alt] + [E]
8. Choose Paste .... [P]

Choose the Paste Special command to specify another Data Type for the embedded object. Then use the Paste button to finish the link.

Mouse Steps

1. Start the application and open the source document.
2. Select the object you want to link.
3. Click on the Edit menu.
4. Click on Copy.
5. Go to the application you want to link to.
6. Open the client document that will accept the linked object; position the cursor.

7. Click on the **E**dit menu.

8. Click on **P**aste.

Choose the Paste Special command to specify another Data Type for the linked object. Then use the Paste button to finish the link.

Objects—Updating Embedded

You can edit any object embedded in a document. (This does not affect the original copy in the source application.) These steps open the object in the source application from the client application.

Keyboard Steps

1. Start the client application and document.

2. Select the embedded object.

3. Pull down the **E**dit menu .... Alt + E

4. Choose the command for editing the **O**bject .... B

The command you select in step 4 will differ depending on the application you're working in.

5. Edit the object in the open application.

6. Pull down the source application's File menu .... `Alt` + `F`
7. Choose Update .... `U`
8. Pull down the source application's File menu .... `Alt` + `F`
9. Choose Exit & Return to *filename* .... `X`

Mouse Steps

1. Start the client application and open the document.
2. Select the embedded object.
3. Click on the Edit menu.
4. Click on ***application*** Object.

The command you select in step 4 will differ depending on the application you're working in.

TIP

5. Edit the object in the open application.
6. Click on the source application's File menu.
7. Click on Update.
8. Click on the source application's File menu.
9. Click on Exit & Return to *filename*.

Objects—Updating Embedded

PIF Editor—386 Enhanced Mode

*When your computer runs non-Windows applications through Windows in 386 Enhanced mode, it can **multitask**, or run more than one application at a time. To do so most effectively, it uses a PIF file for each application to best allocate Windows' resources when running that application. When Windows is in 386 Enhanced mode, the PIF Editor offers these settings:*

PIF Editor offers different options in Standard Mode. See "Mode—Standard PIF."

Setting	Options	Description
Program Filename		Specify the name for the application program file, including a PATH.
Window Title		(Optional) Lets you specify a name for the application's title bar and minimized icon
Optional Parameters		Type in the switches and parameters to use when starting the application (you can use the same ones you would type at the DOS prompt).

Start-up Directory		(Optional) Specify a directory where Windows can find files to start the application (usually the directory containing the program file).
Video Memory	Text	Displays the application in Text mode at startup, using less than 16K of memory
	Low Graphics	Starts the application in a mode comparable to CGA, using less than 32K of memory
	High Graphics	Displays the application in EGA or VGA mode, using up to 128K of memory
Memory Requirements	KB **R**equired	Enter memory needed to start the application.
	KB **D**esired	Enter a maximum of memory the application can use.

continues

PIF Editor—386 Enhanced Mode

Setting	Options	Description
EMS Memory	**K**B Required	Enter the amount of expanded memory needed to start the application.
	KB **L**imit	Sets a maximum of expanded memory the application can use
XMS Memory	KB Re**q**uired	Enter the amount of extended memory needed to start the application.
	KB L**i**mit	Sets a maximum of extended memory the application can use
Display Usage	F**u**ll Screen	Shows the full application screen
	Windowed	Runs the application in a window
Execution	**B**ackground	Lets the application run while another one is active
	Exclusive	Stops other applications while this one is active
Close Window on Exit		Immediately closes the application window (or screen) when you exit the application

*TIP — For many of the memory settings in the preceding list, an entry of -1 provides a special function. See the **H**elp information in PIF Editor to learn more.*

*TIP — Selecting the **A**dvanced button in the PIF Editor displays additional options. Most of the time, there's no need to change these options. Consult the **H**elp system from the PIF Editor or your Windows documentation for more information.*

Keyboard Steps

1. Highlight the Main program group at the Program Manager ...... `Ctrl` + `Tab`

*TIP — You may have to press **Ctrl+Tab** several times to highlight the Main group icon.*

2. Press .... `↵`
3. Highlight the PIF Editor icon .... `←`, `→`, `↑`, or `↓`
4. Press .... `↵`
5. (Optional) Pull down the **F**ile menu .... `Alt` + `F`
6. (Optional) Choose **O**pen .... `O`
7. Type in the file to open .... ***filename.pif***
8. Press .... `↵`

PIF Editor—386 Enhanced Mode

9. Specify the
   options to change .... **Alt** + *selectionletter*
   (if needed, type in) .... *text*
10. Pull down the File menu .... **Alt** + **F**
11. Choose **S**ave or Save **A**s .... **S** or **A**
12. (Optional) Type a file name .... *filename.ext*
13. Press .... ⏎

Mouse Steps

1. At the Program Manager, double-click on the Main program group icon.
2. Double-click on the PIF Editor program-item icon.
3. Click on the File menu.
4. Click on Open.
5. Type in the file to open, as in *filename.pif*.
6. Click on **OK**.
7. Click on the options to change. If necessary, type in *text* in a text box.
8. Click on the File menu.
9. Click on Save or Save As.
10. (Optional) Type a file name, as in *filename.ext*.
11. Click on **OK**.

PIF Editor—Standard Mode

To run DOS applications effectively, Windows uses a PIF file for each application to best allocate Windows' resources (such as memory) when running that application. When Windows is in Standard mode, the PIF Editor offers these settings:

Setting	Options	Description
Program Filename		Specify the name for the application program file, including a PATH.
Window **T**itle		(Optional) Lets you specify a name for the application's title bar and minimized icon
Optional Parameters		Type in the switches and parameters to use when starting the application (you can use the same ones you would type at the DOS prompt).
Start-up Directory		(Optional) Specify a directory where Windows can find files to start the application (usually the directory containing the program file).
Video Mode	Text	Use when application runs in Text mode to save memory for program operation.

continues

Setting	Options	Description
	Graphics/ Multiple Text	Ensures enough memory is available to run the application in a Graphics mode
Memory Requirements	KB **R**equired	Type in the amount of memory needed to start the application.
XMS Memory	KB Re**q**uired	Type in the amount of extended memory needed to start the application.
	KB **L**imit	Sets a maximum of extended memory the application can use
Directly Modifies	COM**1**-**4**	Lets the application use the specified port for communications
	Keyboard	Prevents Windows from responding to the keyboard when the application is active (you must exit to work in Windows)
No Screen **E**xchange		Prevents copying the screen contents to the Clipboard with Alt+Print Screen or the Print Screen key

Prevent Program Switch	Prevents you from switching to another application
No Save Screen	Stops Windows from saving the screen contents when you switch to another application
Close Window on Exit	Immediately closes the application window (or screen) when you exit the application
Reserve Shortcut Keys	Sets the shortcut keys that can only work with the application, not Windows

*The **Directly Modifies** options suspend Windows shortcut keys (such as Ctrl+Esc to display the Task List) when the DOS application they're selected for is active. Be careful when you choose these options.*

Selecting the Advanced button in the PIF Editor displays additional options. Most of the time, there's no need to change these options. Consult the Help system from the PIF Editor or your Windows documentation for more information.

PIF Editor—Standard Mode

Keyboard Steps

1. Highlight the Main program group at the Program Manager ...... **Ctrl** + **Tab**

*You may have to press **Ctrl+Tab** several times to highlight the Main group icon.*

2. Press .... **↵**

3. Highlight the PIF Editor icon .... **←**, **→**, **↑**, or **↓**

4. Press .... **↵**

5. (Optional) Pull down the File menu .... **Alt** + **F**

6. (Optional) Choose **O**pen .... **O**

7. Type in the file to open .... ***filename.pif***

8. Press .... **↵**

9. Specify the options to change .... **Alt** + ***selectionletter***
   (if needed, type in) .... ***text***

10. Pull down the **F**ile menu .... **Alt** + **F**

11. Choose **S**ave or Save **A**s .... **S** or **A**

12. (Optional) Type a file name .... ***filename.ext***

13. Press .... **↵**

Mouse Steps

1. At the Program Manager, double-click on the Main program group icon.
2. Double-click on the PIF Editor program-item icon.
3. Click on the **F**ile menu.
4. Click on **O**pen.
5. Type in the name of the file to open, as in *filename.pif*.
6. Click on **OK**.
7. Click on the options to change. If necessary, type in *text* in a text box.
8. Click on the **F**ile menu.
9. Click on **S**ave or Save **A**s.
10. (Optional) Type a file name, as in *filename.ext*.
11. Click on **OK**.

Printers—Configuring

When you use Control Panel to specify a printer, you can also set settings to determine how Windows uses the capabilities of your Printer. These settings vary for every printer.

*When the Print Manager Window is active, you can also use the **O**ptions Printer Setup command to display the dialog box that lets you configure your printer.*

Keyboard Steps

1. Highlight the Main program group at the Program Manager ...... [Ctrl] + [Tab]
2. Press .... [↵]
3. Highlight the Control Panel program-item icon .... [←], [→], [↑], or [↓]
4. Press .... [↵]
5. Highlight the Printers icon .... [←], [→], [↑], or [↓]
6. Press .... [↵]
7. Choose the printer to configure .... [Alt] + [P]
   [↓] or [↑]
8. (Optional) Choose whether or not to Use Print Manager .... [Alt] + [U]
9. Choose Setup .... [S]
10. Specify the choices .... [Alt] + *selectionletter*
    (if needed) .... [↓], [↑] or
    number
11. Choose Options .... [Alt] + [O]
12. Specify the options.
13. Press .... [↵]

Printers—Configuring

14. Close the dialog box .... ↑ to **OK**
    ↵

15. Close the Printers dialog box .... Tab to Close
    ↵

Mouse Steps

1. At the Program Manager, double-click on the Main program group icon.

2. In the Main program group window, double-click on the Control Panel program-item icon.

3. In the Control Panel window, double-click on the Printers icon.

4. To choose the printer to configure, click on one from the Installed Printers list.

5. (Optional) Click on the Use Print Manager check box.

6. Click on Setup.

7. To specify the choices, click on an option. If needed, type a *number* in the appropriate text box.

8. Click on Options.

9. Specify the options.

10. To close the Options box, click on **OK**.

11. To exit Setup, click on **OK**.

Printers—Configuring

Printers—Selecting Default

*When you install driver files for more than one printer, Windows lets you specify a **default printer**. It will send information to this printer automatically, unless you specify otherwise with the File Printer Setup command in your application.*

Keyboard Steps

1. Highlight the Main program group at the Program Manager ...... `Ctrl` + `Tab`
2. Press .... `↵`
3. Highlight the Control Panel program-item icon .... `←`, `→`, `↑`, or `↓`
4. Press .... `↵`
5. Highlight the Printers icon .... `←`, `→`, `↑`, or `↓`
6. Press .... `↵`
7. Choose the printer to be the default .... `Alt` + `P`
   `↓` or `↑`
8. Choose Set As Default Printer .... `Alt` + `E`
9. Press .... `↵`

Mouse Steps

1. At the Program Manager, double-click on the Main program group icon.

2. In the Main program group window, double-click on the Control Panel program-item icon.

3. In the Control Panel window double-click on the Printers icon.

4. To choose the printer, click on its name in the Installed Printers list.

5. Click on Set As Default Printer.

6. Click on **OK**.

Printers—Selecting Ports

When you select a printer, this setting tells Windows which port it must send the data to. The Device Not Selected option specifies the interval before Print Manager displays a message that it's off-line. Transmission Retry specifies the interval before you see a message that the printer can't hold more information. Fast Printing to Port skips DOS and sends information directly to the printer port.

Keyboard Steps

1. Highlight the Main program group at the Program Manager ...... [Ctrl] + [Tab]

2. Press .... [↵]

3. Highlight the Control Panel program-item icon .... [←], [→], [↑], or [↓]

4. Press .... [↵]

5. Highlight the Printers icon .... [←], [→], [↑], or [↓]

6. Press .... `⏎`
7. Choose the printer to connect .... `Alt` + `P`
   `↓` or `↑`
8. Choose Connect .... `Alt` + `C`
9. Choose the Port .... `Alt` + `P`
   `↓` or `↑`
10. (Optional) Specify a Device
    Not Selected time .... `Alt` + `D`
    number
11. (Optional) Specify a
    Transmission Retry time .... `Alt` + `T`
    number
12. (Optional) Choose Fast Printing
    Direct to Port .... `Alt` + `F`
13. Press .... `⏎`

Mouse Steps

1. At the Program Manager, double-click on the Main program group icon.
2. In the Main program group window, double-click on the Control Panel program-item icon.
3. In the Control Panel window double-click on the Printers icon.
4. To choose the printer, click on its name in the Installed Printers list.
5. Click on Connect.

6. To choose the **P**ort, click on its name in the **P**orts list.

7. (Optional) Click on **D**evice Not Selected time. Type a *number* in the text box.

8. (Optional) Click on **T**ransmission Retry time. Type a *number* in the text box.

9. (Optional) Click on **F**ast Printing Direct to Port.

10. Click on **OK**.

Printing—Deleting a Job

After you've sent a document to the Print Manager for printing, you can delete (cancel) the print operation at any time.

Keyboard Steps

1. Display the Print Manager .... [Alt] + [Tab]

*You may have to press **Alt+Tab** several times.*

2. Highlight the print job .... [↓] or [↑]
3. Choose **D**elete .... [Alt] + [D]
4. Press .... [↵]

Mouse Steps

1. Double-click on the Print Manager icon, or click on the Print Manager window.

2. Click on the print job.
3. Click on **Delete**.
4. Click on **OK**.

Printing—Files

*You can print a document (as long as it's **associated**) directly from the Windows File Manager. See "Files—Associating" for more information about associated files.*

The fastest way to print is to drag the file name from the file list to the Print Manager icon. (Start the Print Manager and minimize it first.)

Keyboard Steps

1. Start the File Manager. (See "File Manager—Starting.")

2. (Optional) Place a disk in the drive to print from.

3. Choose the drive containing the file to print .... **Ctrl** + *driveletter*

*To select drive C:, press **Ctrl+C**; to select drive B:, press **Ctrl+B**; and so on.*

4. Highlight the directory containing the file you want to print .... ↓ or ↑

5. Move to the File list .... `Tab`
6. Highlight the file to print .... `↓`, `↑`, `←`, or `→`
7. Pull down the File menu .... `Alt` + `F`
8. Choose **P**rint .... `P`
9. Press .... `↵`

Mouse Steps

1. Start the File Manager. (See "File Manager—Starting.")
2. (Optional) Place a disk in the disk drive to print from.
3. To select the drive, click on the icon for the drive.
4. To scroll through the directories in the Directory Tree, click on and hold the scroll bar arrows.
5. To select a directory, click on the directory name.
6. Click on the file name.
7. Click on the **F**ile menu.
8. Click on **P**rint.
9. Click on **OK**.

Printing—Pausing a Job

With Print Manager, you can stop a print job temporarily to improve the speed with which the current application is operating.

Keyboard Steps

1. Display the Print Manager .... [Alt] + [Tab]

*You may have to press **Alt+Tab** several times.*

2. Highlight the printer to pause .... [↓] or [↑]
3. Choose **P**ause .... [Alt] + [P]

Mouse Steps

1. Double-click on the Print Manager icon, or click on the Print Manager window.
2. Click on the printer to pause.
3. Click on **P**ause.

Printing—Priorities

Lets you specify how quickly documents print. Note that faster printing (high priority) causes the active application to run more slowly.

Keyboard Steps

1. Display the Print Manager .... [Alt] + [Tab]
2. Pull down the **O**ptions menu .... [Alt] + [O]
3. Choose an option:

   Low Priority .... [L]
   Medium Priority .... [M]
   High Priority .... [H]

Printing—Pausing a Job

Mouse Steps

1. Double-click on the Print Manager icon, or click on the Print Manager window.
2. Click on the **O**ptions menu.
3. Click on an option:

    Low Priority

    Medium Priority

    High Priority

Printing—Resuming a Job

*When you've paused a job in Print Manager, you must **resume** sending it to the printer.*

Keyboard Steps

1. Display the Print Manager .... **Alt** + **Tab**

   *You may have to press **Alt+Tab** several times.*
   TIP

2. Highlight the printer to restart .... **↓** or **↑**
3. Choose **R**esume .... **Alt** + **R**

Mouse Steps

1. Double-click on the Print Manager icon, or click on the Print Manager window.
2. Click on the printer to restart.
3. Click on **R**esume.

Program Groups—Adding

*Just as you store files of similar types together in a directory, Windows lets you organize related programs together in **program groups**. Program groups appear in the Program Manager, where you can minimize them to an icon, open them to a window, or maximize them to full-screen size.*

Keyboard Steps

1. Display the Program Manager .... Alt + Tab

TIP *You may have to press **Alt+Tab** several times. If Alt+Tab doesn't work, use **Alt+Esc**, then press **Enter** to open the minimized icon.*

2. Pull down the File menu .... Alt + F
3. Choose New .... N
4. To choose Program Group,
   press .... G
   ⏎

5. Type a Description (label) .... ***description***
6. (Optional) Select Group File .... Alt + G
7. (Optional) Type a name
   (including a directory PATH)
   for the file that will store
   the program group information
   .... ***drive letter:\directory\filename.grp***

For example, you could type
c:\utilities\virus.grp.

EXAMPLE

8. Press .... ⏎

Mouse Steps

1. Double-click on the Program Manager icon or click on the Program Manager window.

You can also use the Task List to move to the Program Manager. See "Task List."

TIP

2. Click on the **F**ile menu.
3. Click on **N**ew.
4. To choose Program **G**roup, click on (if not already selected) the **Program Group** button then click on **OK**.
5. Type a **D**escription (label), as in ***description***.
6. (Optional) Click on the **G**roup File box.
7. (Optional) Type a name (including a directory PATH) for the file that will store the program group information, as in ***driveletter:\directory\filename.grp***.

Program Groups—Adding 125

EXAMPLE

*For example, you could type **c:\utilities\virus.grp**.*

8. Click on **OK**.

Program Groups—Deleting

Deletes a Program Manager program group icon you no longer need or use, including any program-item icons it contains.

TIP

*The Delete key is a shortcut for the File Delete command. Make sure you know what icon is highlighted in Program Manager before pressing **Delete**.*

Keyboard Steps

1. Display the Program Manager .... **Alt** + **Tab**

TIP

*If Alt+Tab doesn't work, use **Alt+Esc**, then press Enter to open the minimized icon.*

2. Highlight the group to delete .... **Ctrl** + **Tab**
3. Pull down the File menu .... **Alt** + **F**
4. Choose **Delete** .... **D**
5. Press .... **↵**

126 Program Groups—Adding

Mouse Steps

1. Double-click on the Program Manager icon, or click on the Program Manager window.

You can also use the Task List to move to the Program Manager. See "Task List."

2. Highlight the group to delete.
3. Click on the **F**ile menu.
4. Click on **D**elete.
5. Click on **OK**.

Program Manager—Options

*The **O**ptions menu in Program Manager contains three settings that help you work with icons. Use **A**uto Arrange to have Program Manager automatically rearrange a group window's program-item icons when you work with icon placement or window size. When turned on, **M**inimize on Use minimizes the Program Manager whenever you start an application. Once you've arranged the Desktop the way you want it, turn on **S**ave Settings on Exit; the next time you start Windows, the Program Manager windows and icons will be where you placed them.*

*These three commands **toggle** on and off. If a command was off, selecting it turns it on, and vice versa. A checkmark means an option is on.*

Keyboard Steps

1. Display the Program Manager .... `Alt` + `Tab`
2. Pull down the Options menu .... `Alt` + `O`
3. Choose the command you want:

   Auto Arrange .... `A`

   Minimize on Use .... `M`

   Save Settings on Exit .... `S`

Mouse Steps

1. Double-click on the Program Manager icon, or click on the Program Manager window.

You can also use the Task List to move to the Program Manager. See "Task List."

2. Click on the Options menu.
3. Click on the option you want:

   Auto Arrange

   Minimize on Use

   Save Settings on Exit

Program Items—Adding

*Use the steps below to add a **program-item icon** to the selected program group. Program-item icons let you start programs.*

Keyboard Steps

1. Display the Program Manager .... **Alt** + **Tab**
2. Pull down the Window menu .... **Alt** + **W**
3. Choose the number of the group to hold the new program item .... ***number***

EXAMPLE *If you want the Accessories group and it has a 2 beside it on the menu, press 2.*

4. Pull down the File menu .... **Alt** + **F**
5. Choose New .... **N**
6. Choose Program Item .... **I**
7. Press .... **↵**
8. Type a Description (label) .... ***description***
9. Choose Command Line .... **Alt** + **C**
10. Type the name of the file (including a PATH) that starts the program
    ....***drive letter*:*directory**filename.ext***

EXAMPLE *For example, you might type **c:\\quicken\\q.bat** if you're creating a program-item icon for the Quicken program. Use the **B**rowse button if you need to find the file.*

11. (Optional) Choose Working Directory .... **Alt** + **W**

Program Items—Adding 129

12. (Optional) Type the name of the directory containing your data files for this program .... ***directory***

13. (Optional) Choose **S**hortcut Key .... **Alt** + **S**

14. (Optional) Enter a key combination that lets you go to the application when it's running in Windows .... ***key+key***

*You might specify **Alt+Q** for the Quicken program, for example.*

EXAMPLE

15. (Optional) If you want the program to be minimized when you start it, choose **R**un Minimized .... **Tab**
    Space

16. (Optional) Choose Change **I**con .... **Alt** + **I**

*Windows may display a message telling you there are no icons for the selected file. Press **Enter** to continue.*

TIP

17. (Optional) In the **F**ilename text box, type .... ***PROGMAN.EXE*** or ***MORICONS.DLL***

18. (Optional) Select an icon from
    the Current icon list .... Tab
    ← or →
19. (Optional) Press .... ↵
20. Press .... ↵

Mouse Steps

1. Double-click on the Program Manager icon, or click on the Program Manager window.

You can also use the Task List to move to the Program Manager. See "Task List."

TIP

2. Click on the **W**indow menu.
3. Click on the number of the group to hold the new program-item.
4. Click on the **F**ile menu.
5. Click on **N**ew.
6. Click on Program Item.
7. Click on **OK**.
8. Type a **D**escription (label), as in ***description***.
9. Click on **C**ommand Line.
10. Type the name of the file (including a PATH) that starts the program, as in ***driveletter:\directory\filename.ext***.

Program Items—Adding

EXAMPLE *For example, you might type **c:\quicken\q.bat** if you're creating a program-item icon for the Quicken program. Use the Browse button if you need to find the file.*

11. (Optional) Click on **W**orking Directory.

12. (Optional) Type the name of the directory containing your data files for this program, as in **\directory**.

13. (Optional) Click on **S**hortcut Key.

14. (Optional) Type a key combination that lets you go to the application when it's running in Windows, as in **key+key**.

*You might specify **Alt+Q** for the Quicken program, for example.*

EXAMPLE

15. (Optional) If you want the program to be minimized when you start it, click on **R**un Minimized.

16. (Optional) Click on Change **I**con.

*Windows may display a message telling you there are no icons for the selected file. Press **Enter** to continue.*

TIP

17. (Optional) In the **F**ilename text box, type ....***PROGMAN.EXE*** or ***MORICONS.DLL***.

132 Program Items—Adding

18. (Optional) To select an icon, click on one from the Current icon choices.

19. (Optional) Click on **OK**.

20. Click on **OK**.

Program Items—Deleting

You can delete any program-item icon you no longer use. This helps keep the Desktop neat and uncluttered.

Keyboard Steps

1. Display the Program Manager .... Alt + Tab
2. Pull down the Window menu .... Alt + W
3. Choose the number of the group that holds the program-item icon .... ***number***

EXAMPLE *If you want the Accessories group and it has a 2 beside it on the menu, press 2.*

4. Highlight the name of the icon to delete .... ← or →, ↑ or ↓
5. Pull down the File menu .... Alt + F
6. Choose Delete .... D
7. Press .... Y or ↵

Program Items—Deleting

Mouse Steps

1. Double-click on the Program Manager icon, or click on the Program Manager window.

You can also use the Task List to move to the Program Manager. See "Task List."

TIP

2. Click on the **W**indow menu.
3. Click on the number of the group that holds the program-item.

*If you want the Accessories group, and it has a 2 beside it on the menu, click on **2**.*

EXAMPLE

4. Click on the icon to delete.
5. Click on the **F**ile menu.
6. Click on **D**elete.
7. Click on **OK**.

*The Delete key is a shortcut for the File Delete command. Make sure you know what icon is highlighted in Program Manager before pressing **Delete**.*

TIP

Program Items—Moving

You have the option of moving program-item icons from one program group to another to rearrange the Desktop.

Keyboard Steps

1. Display the Program Manager .... `Alt` + `Tab`
2. Pull down the Window menu .... `Alt` + `W`
3. Choose the number for the group that holds the program item .... ***number***

EXAMPLE

If you want the Accessories group and it has a 2 beside it on the menu, press 2.

4. Highlight the name of the icon to move .... `←`, `→`, `↑`, or `↓`
5. Pull down the File menu .... `Alt` + `F`
6. Choose Move .... `M`
7. Highlight the name of the program group to move the icon to .... `↓` or `↑`
8. Press .... `↵`

Mouse Steps

1. Double-click on the Program Manager icon, or click on the Program Manager window.

You can also use the Task List to move to the Program Manager. See "Task List."

2. Double-click on the program group icon for the group that contains the icon, or click on **Window** and then click on the number for the appropriate group.

3. Drag the program-item icon to another program group icon.

Programs—Quitting

You can quit any Windows application you're running by choosing the application's Exit or Quit command. (These commands vary from application to application.) You can also use the program's Control menu, as described here.

*For DOS applications running in full-screen mode, you must use the program's own **Exit** or **Quit** command.*

Keyboard Steps

1. Pull down the application's
   Control menu .... Alt + Space
2. Choose **C**lose C

Mouse Steps

1. Double-click on the Control menu box (upper left corner of the application's window).

Programs—Starting

The program-item icons in the Program Manager represent applications. Selecting a program-item icon from a program group starts the application it represents.

Keyboard Steps

1. Display the Program Manager .... [Alt] + [Tab]
2. Pull down the Window menu .... [Alt] + [W]
3. Choose the number for the program group that holds the program-item icon .... ***number***

EXAMPLE

If you want the Accessories group, and it has a 2 beside it on the menu, press 2.

4. Highlight the name of the icon to start .... [←], [→], [↑], or [↓]
5. Press .... [↵]

Mouse Steps

1. Double-click on the Program Manager icon, or click on the Program Manager window.

You can also use the Task List to move to the Program Manager. See "Task List."

2. Double-click on the program item icon for the application to start.

Properties—Files

*The File Manager lets you assign certain **properties** to files. Some of these properties are commonly referred to as **attributes** for the files. Following are the property options in File Manager, and what each does when you assign it to a file.*

Property	Description
Read Only	Lets you open the file to view it, but prevents changes
Archive	Displays an **A** in file listings for each file that has changed since it was last backed up
Hidden	Prevents a file from being displayed in directory listings
System	Indicates DOS system files, and prevents them from being displayed in DOS directory listings

Keyboard Steps

1. Display the File Manager. (See "File Manager—Starting.")

2. (Optional) Place the disk holding the file in the disk drive.

3. (Optional) Choose the
   drive holding the file .... `Ctrl` + ***driveletter***

   EXAMPLE
   *To select drive C:, press **Ctrl+C**; to select drive B:, press **Ctrl+B**; and so on.*

4. Highlight the name of the directory
   holding the file .... `↓` or `↑`

5. Select the file
   (see "Files—Selecting").

6. Pull down the File menu .... `Alt` + `F`

7. Choose Properties .... `T`

8. Press .... `Alt` + `F`

9. Type a new file name .... ***filename.ext***

10. Press .... `Alt` + `P`

11. Type a new PATH
    location .... ***diskletter:\directory***

12. Specify the attributes you want:

    Read Only .... `Alt` + `R`

    Archive .... `Alt` + `A`

    Hidden .... `Alt` + `I`

    System .... `Alt` + `S`

13. Press .... `↵`

Properties—Files

Mouse Steps

1. Double-click on the File Manager icon, or click on the File Manager window.

You can also use the Task List to move to the Program Manager. See "Task List."

2. (Optional) Place the disk containing the file in the disk drive.

3. (Optional) To select the drive with the file, click on the icon for the drive.

4. To scroll through the directories in the Directory Tree, click on and hold the scroll bar arrows.

5. To select a directory, click on the directory name.

6. Select the file (see "Files—Selecting").

7. Click on the File menu.

8. Click on Properties.

9. Drag to highlight the File Name.

10. Type a new file name, as in ***filename.ext***.

11. Drag to highlight the Path name.

12. Type a new PATH location, as in ***diskletter:\directory***.

13. Click on options that specify the attributes you want:

Read Only

Archive

Hidden

System

14. Click on **OK**.

Properties—Program

You can change the properties—attributes such as the icon name and the icon—for any program-item icon in the Program Manager.

Keyboard Steps

1. Display the Program Manager .... `Alt` + `Tab`
2. Pull down the **W**indow menu .... `Alt` + `W`
3. Choose the number of the group that holds the program item .... ***number***

EXAMPLE
If you want the Accessories group, and it has a 2 beside it on the menu, press 2.

4. Highlight the program item ... `←`, `→`, `↑`, or `↓`
5. Pull down the **F**ile menu .... `Alt` + `F`
6. Choose **P**roperties .... `P`
7. Type a **D**escription (label) .... ***description***
8. Choose **C**ommand Line .... `Alt` + `C`

9. Type the name of the file (including a PATH) that starts the program ....***driveletter*:*directory**filename.ext***

EXAMPLE

For example, you might type ***c:\\quicken\\q.bat*** *if you're creating a program-item icon for the Quicken program. Use the **Browse** button if you need to find the file.*

10. (Optional) Choose **W**orking Directory .... Alt + W

11. (Optional) Type the name of the directory that holds your data files for this program .... ***directory***

12. (Optional) Choose **S**hortcut Key .... Alt + S

13. (Optional) Type a key combination that lets you go to the application when it's running in Windows .... ***key+key***

EXAMPLE

*You might specify **Alt+Q** for the Quicken program, for example.*

14. (Optional) If you want the program to be minimized when you start it, choose **R**un Minimized .... Tab
Space

Properties—Program

15. (Optional) Choose Change Icon .... `Alt` + `I`

*Windows may display a message telling you there are no icons for the selected file. Press **Enter** to continue.*

16. In the Filename text
    box, type .... ***PROGMAN.EXE***
    or ***MORICONS.DLL***

17. Select an icon from
    the Current icon list .... `Tab`
    `←` or `→`

18. Press .... `↵`

19. Press .... `↵`

Mouse Steps

1. Double-click on the Program Manager icon, or click on the Program Manager window.

You can also use the Task List to move to the Program Manager. See "Task List."

2. Click on the Window menu.

3. Click on the number of the group that holds the program-item.

4. Click on the File menu.

5. Click on Properties.

6. Type a Description (label), as in ***description***.

Properties—Program

7. Click on Command Line.

8. Type the name of the file (including a PATH) that starts the program, as in ***driveletter:\directory\filename.ext***.

*For example, you might type **c:\quicken\q.bat** if you're creating a program-item icon for the Quicken program. Use the **B**rowse button if you need to find the file.*

9. (Optional) Click on **W**orking Directory.

10. (Optional) Type the name of the directory containing your data files for this program, as in ***\directory***.

11. (Optional) Click on **S**hortcut Key.

12. (Optional) Type a key combination that lets you go to the application when it's running in Windows, as in ***key+key***.

*You might specify **Alt+Q** for the Quicken program, for example.*

13. (Optional) If you want the program to be minimized when you start it, click on **R**un Minimized.

14. (Optional) Click on Change **I**con.

*Windows may display a message telling you there are no icons for the selected file. Press **Enter** to continue.*

15. (Optional) In the Filename text box, type **PROGMAN.EXE** or **MORICONS.DLL**.

16. (Optional) To select an icon, click on one from the Current icon choices.

17. Click on **OK**.

18. Click on **OK**.

Serial Ports—Configuring

*Your mouse, modem, and maybe even your printer (all called **devices**) are connected to COM (serial) ports on your system. With the Control Panel, you can change the following settings for each COM port attached to your system.*

Setting	Description
Baud Rate	Tells Windows how fast the device carries data
Data Bits	Tells Windows the number of data bits used for each character (*byte*) transferred
Parity	Chooses error-checking
Stop Bits	Sets a time to space each character
Flow Control	Lets you tell Windows if your hardware controls the flow of data

Serial Ports—Configuring 145

Check the documentation for the device to determine how you should configure the COM port it's connected to.

There are Advanced port options; in general, however, it's not recommended to change them. See the Windows Help system if you think you may need to change the Advanced settings for a port.

Keyboard Steps

1. Display the Program Manager .... [Alt] + [Tab]

*You may have to press **Alt+Tab** several times.*

2. Highlight the Main program group at the Program Manager ...... [Ctrl] + [Tab]

*You may have to press **Ctrl+Tab** several times to highlight the Main group icon.*

3. Press .... [↵]
4. Highlight the Control Panel icon .... [←], [→], [↑], or [↓]
5. Press .... [↵]
6. Highlight the Ports icon .... [←], [→], [↑], or [↓]

Serial Ports—Configuring

7. Press .... `↵`
8. Select a port .... `Alt` + *number*
9. Choose Settings .... `Alt` + `S`
10. Select each option .... `Alt` + *selectionletter* `↑` or `↓`
11. Press .... `↵`

Mouse Steps

1. Double-click on the Program Manager icon, or click on the Program Manager window.

2. At the Program Manager, double-click on the Main program group icon.

3. Double-click on the Control Panel program-item icon.

4. Double-click on the Ports icon.

5. Click on the icon for the port to configure.

6. Click on Settings.

7. To select each option, click on the down arrow beside it, then click on a choice from the list.

8. Click on **OK**.

Sound—Configuring

You can assign a sound (created by .WAV files) rather than a beep to each Windows event (starting, exiting, etc.) if you have a sound card installed with your system.

Microsoft also offers a sound driver file called PC Speaker to let almost any system play back the .WAV files (four of them) that come with Windows. Contact Microsoft Customer Sales and Service/One Microsoft Way/Redmond, WA 98052-6399.

*Use the **Test** button to hear the sounds you're selecting.*

Keyboard Steps

1. Display the Program Manager .... **Alt** + **Tab**

*You may have to press **Alt+Tab** several times.*

2. Highlight the Main program group at the Program Manager ...... **Ctrl** + **Tab**

*You may have to press **Ctrl+Tab** several times to highlight the Main group icon.*

3. Press .... ⏎

4. Highlight the Control Panel icon .... ←, →, ↑, or ↓

148 Sound—Configuring

5. Press .... [↵]
6. Highlight the Sound icon .... [←], [→], [↑], or [↓]
7. Press .... [↵]
8. Highlight the Event to
   change the sound for .... [↓] or [↑]
9. Select Files .... [Alt] + [F]
10. Highlight the file name .... [↓] or [↑]
11. Choose Enable
    System Sounds .... [Alt] + [N]
12. Press .... [↵]

Mouse Steps

1. Double-click on the Program Manager icon, or click on the Program Manager window.

2. At the Program Manager, double-click on the Main program group icon.

3. Double-click on the Control Panel program-item icon.

4. Double-click on the Sound icon.

5. In the Events list, click on the event to change the sound for.

6. In the Files list, click on the .WAV file name.

7. (Optional) Click on Enable System Sounds.

8. Click on **OK**.

Sound—Configuring

Task List

The Windows Task List offers an easy way to switch between and arrange applications that are running or minimized to an icon. Here are the options it offers.

Command Button	Description
Switch To	Choose to change to the application highlighted in the list.
End Task	Closes (exits or quits) the application highlighted in the list
Cascade	Overlaps the windows for all applications that are running
Tile	Equally sizes the windows for all applications that are running, to fill the screen
Arrange Icons	Arranges the icons for all applications minimized to icons
Cancel	Closes the Task List dialog box

Keyboard Steps

1. Display the Task List .... **Ctrl** + **Esc**
2. (If necessary) Highlight another application name .... **↓** or **↑**
3. Select a button .... ***selectionletter***

Mouse Steps

1. Display the Task List by pressing Ctrl + Esc.
2. (If necessary) click on another application name.
3. Click on a command button.

Double-clicking on an application's name switches you to it automatically.

TrueType—Setting Options

Loading TrueType fonts requires large amounts of computer memory, so you may want to turn them off. Or you may want to see only TrueType fonts in the font list for your application.

Keyboard Steps

1. Highlight the Main program group at the Program Manager ...... `Ctrl` + `Tab`

*You may have to press **Ctrl+Tab** several times to highlight the Main group icon.*

2. Press .... `↵`
3. Highlight the Control Panel icon .... `←`, `→`, `↑`, or `↓`
4. Press .... `↵`
5. Highlight the Fonts icon .... `←`, `→`, `↑`, or `↓`
6. Press .... `↵`
7. Select **T**rueType .... `Alt` + `T`
8. To turn TrueType fonts on or off, choose **E**nable TrueType Fonts .... `Alt` + `E`

9. Select whether or not to display only TrueType fonts in application menus .... Alt + S

10. Press .... ⏎

Mouse Steps

1. At the Program Manager, double-click on the Main program group icon.

2. Double-click on the Control Panel program-item icon.

3. Double-click on the Fonts icon.

4. Click on **T**rueType.

5. To turn TrueType fonts on or off, click on **E**nable TrueType Fonts.

6. To select whether or not to display only TrueType fonts in the application's Font menus, click on **S**how Only TrueType Fonts in Applications.

7. Click on **OK**.

Windows—Arranging

*Lets you specify how all the open windows should appear on-screen in the Program Manager or File Manager. Choose **C**ascade to overlap the windows, with the active window on top. Choose **T**ile to size all windows equally to fill the screen.*

TrueType—Setting Options

Keyboard Steps

1. Pull down the Window menu .... `Alt` + `W`
2. Choose Cascade or Tile .... `C` or `T`

***Shift+F5** is a shortcut for Window Cascade. **Shift+F4** is a shortcut for Window Tile.*

Mouse Steps

1. Click on the Window menu.
2. Click on Cascade or Tile.

Windows—Closing

You can use the Control menu to close any application window, program group window, or directory window.

Keyboard Steps

1. Select the window to close.
   (See "Windows—Selecting.")

2. Display the Control menu:

   For an application or the
   Program Manager itself .... `Alt` + `Space`

   For a program group or
   directory window .... `Alt` + `-`

Alt+Spacebar *will open the Control menu for the Program manager. If you close the Program Manager, you are exiting Windows.*

3. Choose Close .... [C]

Mouse Steps

1. Select the window to close (see "Windows—Selecting").

2. Display the Control menu by clicking on the Control menu box in the window's upper left corner.

3. Click on Close.

Double-clicking on a window's Control menu box closes it.

Windows—Maximizing

Enlarges a window to full-screen size.

Keyboard Steps

1. Select the window.
   (See "Windows—Selecting.")

2. Display the Control menu:

   For an application or the
   Program Manager itself .... [Alt] + [Space]

For a program group
or directory window .... Alt + -

3. Choose Maximize X

Mouse Steps

1. Select the window (see "Windows—Selecting").

2. Display the Control menu by clicking on the Control menu box (window's upper left corner).

3. Click on Maximize.

To maximize a window, click on the maximize button (labeled with the up arrow) in its upper right corner, or double-click on its title bar.

Windows—Minimizing

Shrinks a window to an icon at the bottom of the screen.

Keyboard Steps

1. Select the window.
   (See "Windows—Selecting.")

2. Display the Control menu by:

   For an application or the
   Program Manager itself .... Alt + Space

   For a program group
   or directory window .... Alt + -

3. Choose Minimize .... N

Mouse Steps

1. Select the window. (See "Windows—Selecting.")

2. Display the Control menu by clicking on the Control menu box (window's upper left corner).

3. Click on Minimize.

To maximize a window, click on the minimize button (labeled with the down arrow) in its upper right corner, or double-click on its title bar.

Windows—Moving

Any window that's not displayed at full-screen size (maximized) can be moved around.

Keyboard Steps

1. Select the window.
   (See "Windows—Selecting.")

2. Display the Control menu:

   For an application or the
   Program Manager itself .... `Alt` + `Space`

   For a program group
   or directory window .... `Alt` + `-`

3. Choose Move .... `M`

4. Position the window
   on-screen .... `↑`, `↓`, `→`, `←`

5. Press .... `↵`

Windows—Minimizing

Mouse Steps

1. Point to the window's title bar.
2. Drag the window into position.

Windows—Restoring

When you make a window smaller or minimize it, you can restore it to its previous size.

Keyboard Steps

1. Select the window.
   (See "Windows—Selecting.")

2. Display the Control menu:

   For an application or the
   Program Manager itself .... **Alt** + **Space**

   For a program group or
   directory window .... **Alt** + **-**

3. Choose **R**estore .... **R**

Mouse Steps

1. Select the window. (See "Windows—Selecting.")

2. Display the Control menu by clicking on the Control menu box (window's upper-left corner).

3. Click on **R**estore.

Double-clicking on a window's title bar can also restore it.

Windows—Selecting

You can select program group windows and icons in the Program Manager, and directory windows in File Manager.

Keyboard Steps

*Note that these steps only work from the Program Manager and File Manager. To switch to another application from an open application, use **Alt+Tab**, or **Alt+Esc** and **Enter**.*

1. Press .... Ctrl + Tab

*Use **Ctrl+Tab** as many times as needed to get to the correct window.*

Mouse Steps

1. Click on the window you want to select.

Windows—Sizing

You can resize any window that's not displayed at full-screen size.

Keyboard Steps

1. Select the window.
   (See "Windows—Selecting.")

158 Windows—Selecting

2. Display the Control menu:

   For an application or the
   Program Manager itself .... **Alt** + **Space**

   For a program group or
   directory window .... **Alt** + **-**

3. Choose Size .... **S**

4. Select a window border .... ***arrow keys***

5. Move the window border ..... **↓**, **↑**, **←**, or **→**

6. Press .... **↵**

7. Repeat steps 2-6 as needed.

Mouse Steps

1. Select the window (see "Windows—Selecting").

2. Point to a window border or corner.

3. Drag the window border or corner.

Windows—Sizing

Index

Symbols

* (asterisk) wild-card character
  renaming multiple files, 63-64
  searching for files, 67-68
? (question mark) wild-card character
  renaming multiple files, 63-64
  searching for files, 67-68
386-Enhanced mode, 95-98
  icon, 97
  options, 96-97
  PIF Editor, 104-108

A

accessing Program Manager Task List, 125
active applications, changing, 3-5
All File Details (File Manager's View menu) command, 71
applets, 1
  Clipboard Viewer, 5-14
  Control Panel, 19-23, 44-47, 75-80, 87-91
  Setup, 1-3, 48-49, 80-82
applications, 52
  adding to Windows, 128-133
  associating files, 53-55
  changing Task List, 150
  closing Task List, 150
  displaying, 105
  DOS
    changing settings, 39-42
    running, 109-113
  installing, 1-3
  ports in use, 96
  quitting, 136-137
  running from File Manager, 65-67
  starting, 137-138
  switching, 3-5
    fast switching, 20
  windows, closing, 153-154
Archive file property, 141
Arrange Icons (Window menu) command, 85
arranging
  icons, 150
  windows, 152-153
assigning sounds, 147-151
Associate (File Manager's File menu) command, 54-55
associating files with applications, 53-55
asterisk (*) wild-card character
  renaming multiple files, 63-64
  searching for files, 67-68
Auto (Clipboard Viewer's Display menu) command, 5-6
Auto Arrange (Options menu) command, 127

B

background
  patterns, choosing, 20
  wallpaper, choosing, 21
  Windows, 96
baud rate, 145
Bitmap (Clipboard Viewer's Display menu) command, 5-6
blink rate, cursor, 21
borders, setting width, 21

branches
  collapsing, 26
  expanding, 26-28
breaking links, 94
buttons, mouse, switching, 98
By File Type (File Manager's View menu) command, 73

C

canceling
  Clipboard-contents deletions, 9
  links, 94
  print jobs, 119-120
Cascade (Window menu) command, 153
cascading windows, 150, 153
Change System Settings (Setup's Options menu) command, 48-49, 81-82
Clear Clipboard dialog box, 9-10
clearing, *see* deleting
clicking mouse, 98
client documents (OLE), 92
Clipboard
  copying or cutting to, 6-7
  deleting contents, 8-9
  files, opening, 9-10
  pasting from, 10-11
  saving contents as files, 11-13
  starting, 13-14
  viewing contents, 5-6
Clipboard Viewer icon, 13-14
closing applications, 150-154
.CLP file extension, 9, 11
Collapse Branch (File Manager's Tree menu) command, 26
Color dialog box
  changing screen-element colors, 14-16
  choosing color schemes, 16-17
  creating colors, 17-19
  opening, 19-20

Color icon, 19-20
color schemes
  changing for screen elements, 14-16
  choosing, 16-17
  creating, 14, 17-19
COM Ports
  options, 96
  settings, 145-146
  sharing, 95
commands
  All File Details (File Manager's View menu), 71
  Arrange Icons (Window menu), 85
  Associate (File Manager's File menu), 54-55
  Auto (Clipboard Viewer's Display menu), 5-6
  Auto Arrange (Options menu), 127
  Bitmap (Clipboard Viewer's Display menu), 5-6
  By File Type (File Manager's View menu), 73
  Cascade (Window menu), 153
  Change System Settings (Setup's Options menu), 48-49, 81-82
  Collapse Branch (File Manager's Tree menu), 26
  Confirmation (File Manager's Options menu), 50, 59
  Copy (Edit menu), 7, 92
  Copy (File Manager's File menu), 56-57
  Copy Disk (File Manager's Disk menu), 33-36
  Create Directory (File Manager's File menu), 24-25
  Cut (Edit menu), 7
  Delete (Clipboard Viewer's Edit menu), 8-9

Delete (File Manager's File menu), 58-59
Directory Only (File Manager's View menu), 71
Exit (Options menu), 2, 3
Expand All (File Manager's Tree menu), 27-28
Expand Branch (File Manager's Tree menu), 27-28
Expand One Level (File Manager's Tree menu), 27-28
Font (File Manager's Options menu), 50-51
Fonts (application's Control menu), 43
Format Disk (File Manager's Disk menu), 37-39
Help, 82-85
High Priority (Options menu), 122
Indicate Expandable Branches (File Manager's Tree menu), 28
Links (Edit menu), 94
Low Priority (Options menu), 122
Maximize (Control menu), 155
Medium Priority (Options menu), 122
Minimize (Control menu), 156
Minimize on use (File Manager's Options menu), 51, 127
Move (File Manager's File menu), 60-61
Name (File Manager's View menu), 71
New Window (File Manager's Window menu), 31-32
Object (Edit menu), 102
OEM Text (Clipboard Viewer's Display menu), 5-6

Open (Clipboard Viewer's File menu), 9-10
Partial File Details (File Manager's View menu), 71-72
Paste (Edit menu), 11
Paste Link (Edit menu), 92
Paste Special (Edit menu), 11, 92
Print (File menu), 121
Printer (Options menu), 113
Printer Setup (File menu), 116
Properties (File menu), 139
Refresh (Window menu), 32
Rename (File Manager's File menu), 63-65
Restore (Control menu), 157
Run (File Manager's File menu), 66
Save As (Clipboard Viewer's File menu), 12-13
Save Settings on Exit (File Manager's Options menu, 51, 128
Search (File Manager's File menu), 67-68
Select Files (File Manager's File menu), 69
Set Up Applications (Setup's Options menu), 1-3
Settings (application's Control menu), 39-42
Sort by Date (File Manager's View menu), 72
Sort by Name (File Manager's View menu), 72
Sort by Size (File Manager's View menu), 72
Sort by Type (File Manager's View menu), 72
Split (File Manager's View menu), 30-31
Status Bar (File Manager's Options menu), 51

Switch To (Control menu), 4-5
Text (Clipboard Viewer's Display menu), 5-6
Tile (Window menu), 153
toggles, 73, 127
Tree and Directory (File Manager's View menu), 71
Tree Only (File Manager's View menu), 71
Update (File menu), 103
configuration
  serial ports, 145-147
  printers, 113-115
  sound, 147-151
Confirmation (File Manager's Options menu) command, 50, 59
context-sensitive help, 82-84
Control menu, switching applications, 4-5
Control Panel applet
  Color icon, 19-20
  Desktop icon, 22-23
  Double Click Speed, 98
  Drivers icon, 44-47
  Fonts icon, 75-80
  International icon, 87-90
  Keyboard icon, 91
  Mouse Tracking Speed, 98
  Mouse Trails, 98
  Swap Left/Right Buttons, 98
Control Panel icon, 19, 22, 44, 75-78, 88-90
Copy (Edit menu) command, 7, 92
Copy (File Manager's File menu) command, 56-57
Copy Disk (File Manager's Disk menu) command, 33-36
copying
  disks, 33-36
  files, 55-57
  to Clipboard, 6-7

Create Directory (File Manager's File menu) command, 24-25
creating
  .CLP files, 11-13
  color schemes, 14, 17-19
  directories, 23-25
  links, 92-93
  program-item icons, 128-133
cursor
  blink rate, setting, 21
  movement rate, modifying, 90
customizing
  mouse, 98-100
  Program Manager, 127-159
Cut (Edit menu) command, 7
cutting
  to Clipboard, 6-7
  see also moving

D

data bits, 145
data types, linking objects, 92
default printers, selecting, 116-117
Delete (Clipboard Viewer's Edit menu) command, 8-9
Delete (File Manager's File menu) command, 58-59
deleting
  Clipboard contents, 8-9
  files, 58-59
  fonts from system, 78-80
  print jobs, 119-120
  program groups (Program Manager), 126-127
  program items, 133-134
desktop
  arranging icons, 85
  customizing, 20-23
Desktop icon, 22-23

device drivers
　changing hardware settings, 80-82
　installing, 44-47
　video, choosing, 48-49
devices, ports, configuring, 145-147
dialog boxes
　Clear Clipboard, 9-10
　Color, 14-20
　Setup, 45-47
directories
　choosing, 28-29
　creating, 23-25
　displaying subdirectories, 26-28
　moving files between, 60-62
　renaming, 62-65
　viewing contents, 25-26
Directory Only (File Manager's View menu) command, 71
Directory Tree
　choosing drives and directories, 28-29
　collapsing levels, 26
　expanding levels, 26-28
　resizing in directory windows, 30-31
　viewing multiple parts, 31-32
directory windows
　adjusting split widths, 30-31
　arranging, *see* windows
　closing, *see* windows
　opening multiple, 31-32
　refreshing, 32-33
　selecting, 158
disks
　copying, 33-36
　formatting, 36-39
　moving files between, 60-62
displaying
　applications, 105
　grids, 21
　subdirectories, 26-28

documents
　client, 92
　pasting to, 10-11
　source, 92-94
DOS applications
　settings, changing, 39-42
　font sizes, changing, 42-43
　running, 109-113
Double Click Speed (Control Panel), 98
double-clicking, starting files/applications, 66-67
driver files, *see* device drivers
drivers, sound, 148
Drivers icon, 44-47
drives, choosing, 28-29
duplicating, *see* copying

E

editing objects
　embedded, 102-103
　linked, 93
editors, PIF, 104-108
EGA mode, displaying applications, 105
embedded objects, 100-102
　editing, 102-103
　updating, 102-103
erasing, *see* deleting
events, assigning sounds, 147-151
executable files, starting, 65-67
Exit (Options menu) command, 2-3, 136
Expand All (File Manager's Tree menu) command, 27-28
Expand Branch (File Manager's Tree menu) command, 27-28
Expand One Level (File Manager's Tree menu) command, 27-28
expanding Directory Tree levels, 26-28

F

fast switching between applications, 20
File list
   customizing, 70-75
   refreshing, 32-33
   resizing in directory windows, 30-31
File Manager
   customizing, 50-52
   directories
      choosing, 28-29
      creating, 23-25
      displaying subdirectories, 26-28
      renaming, 62-65
      viewing contents, 25-26
   directory windows
      adjusting split widths, 30-31
      opening multiple, 31-32
      selecting, 158
   disks
      copying, 33-36
      formatting, 36-39
   drives, choosing, 28-29
   files
      associating with applications, 53-55
      copying, 55-57
      deleting, 58-59
      executable, starting, 65-67
      moving between disks or directories, 60-62
      opening, 65-67
      properties, 138-141
      renaming, 62-65
      searching for, 67-68
      selecting, 69-70
      viewing, 70-75
   options, file properties, 138
   printing from, 120
   starting, 52-53
File Manager icon, 53
files
   associating with applications, 53-55
   copying, 55-57
   deleting, 58-59
   driver, *see* device drivers
   executable, starting, 65-67
   extensions
      .CLP, 9, 11
      for executable files, 65
   moving between disks or directories, 60-62
   opening
      by starting associated applications, 65-67
      from Clipboard, 9-10
   PIF, 104
   printing, 120-121
   properties, 138-141
   renaming, 62-65
   saving Clipboard contents as, 11-13
   searching for, 67-68
   selecting, 69-70
   viewing, 70-75
      in multiple directories, 31-32
finding, *see* searching for
flow control, 145
Font (File Manager's Options menu) command, 50-51
fonts
   deleting from system, 78-80
   installing, 75-78
   sizes, changing, 42-43
Fonts (application's Control menu) command, 43
Fonts icon, 75-80
foreground Windows, 96
foreign languages, setting options for, 87-90

Format Disk (File Manager's Disk menu) command, 37-39
formats, Clipboard contents, changing, 5-6
formatting disks, 36-39

G

graphics
  copying or cutting to Clipboard, 6-7
  pasting from Clipboard, 10-11
grids, displaying, 21

H

hardware, changing settings, 80-82
Help system, 82-84
Hidden file property, 141
High Priority (Options menu) command, 122
highlighting files, 69-70

I

icons, 85
  386-Enhanced, 97
  arranging, 85, 150
  Clipboard Viewer, 13-14
  Color, 19-20
  Control Panel, 19, 22, 44, 75-78, 88-90
  Desktop, 22-23
  Drivers, 44-47
  File Manager, 53
  Fonts, 75-80
  International, 87-90
  Keyboard, 91
  Main program group, 13
  Printers, 117
  program groups, 124-126
  program-item, 1, 128-133
  selecting, 86-87
  setting spacing, 21
  Windows Setup, 1, 48, 80-81
  wrapping titles, 21
Indicate Expandable Branches (File Manager's Tree menu) command, 28
installing
  applications, 1-3
  device drivers, 44-47
  driver files, printers, 116
  fonts, 75-78
International icon, 87-90

J-K

keyboard, customizing, 90-91
Keyboard icon, 91
keyboard shortcuts, suspending, 111
keys, repeat rates, modifying, 90

L

languages, foreign, 87-90
linking
  breaking links, 94
  creating links, 92-93
  objects
    automatic update, 93-94
    changing links, 94
    Data Types, 92
    editing, 93
    locked update, 94
    manual update, 94
  updating links, 93-95
linking files to applications, 53-55
Links (Edit menu) command, 94
locking updated linked objects, 94
Low Priority (Options menu) command, 122

M

Main program group icon, 13
Maximize (Control menu)
   command, 155
maximizing windows, 154-155
Medium Priority (Options menu)
   command, 122
memory, 97
   see also virtual memory
menus
   Options (File Manager), 50-51
   View (File Manager), 70-74
Minimize (Control menu)
   command, 156
Minimize on use (File Manager's
   Options menu) command,
   51, 127
minimizing windows, 155-156
   Program Manager, 127
modes
   386-Enhanced, 95-98
      PIF Editor, 104-108
   Standard, 109-113
modifying keyboard, 91
monitor drivers, *see* video drivers
mouse
   buttons, switching, 98
   customizing, 98-100
   double clicking, 98
   pointer, speed, 98
   trails, 98
Mouse Tracking Speed (Control
   Panel), 98
Mouse Trails (Control Panel), 98
Move (File Manager's File menu)
   command, 60-61
moving
   files between disks or
      directories, 60-62
   program item icons, 135-136
   windows, 156-157
   see also cutting; pasting
multitasking, 104

N-O

Name (File Manager's View menu)
   command, 71
New Window (File Manager's
   Window menu) command,
   31-32

Object (Edit menu) command, 102
Object Linking and Embedding,
   see OLE
objects, 92
   embedded, 100-102
      editing, 102-103
      updating, 102-103
   linking
      automatic update, 93-94
      breaking links, 94
      changing links, 94
      data types, 92
      editing, 93
      locked update, 94
      manual update, 94
   source application, opening,
      102
OEM Text (Clipboard Viewer's
   Display menu) command,
   5-6
OLE (Object Linking and
   Embedding), 92, 100-102
   canceling links, 94
   changing links, 94
   client documents, 92
   linking
      automatic update, 94
      locking, 94
      manual update, 94
   source documents, 92-94
   see also objects; linking
Open (Clipboard Viewer's File
   menu) command, 9-10

opening
 Clipboard files, 9-10
 Color dialog box, 19-20
 files, 65-67
 multiple directory windows, 31-32
options
 386-Enhanced mode, 96-97
 COM ports, 96
 File Manager file properties, 138
 PIF Editor
  386-Enhanced mode, 104-106
  Standard mode, 109-111
 Program Manager, 127-128
 TrueType, 151-152
Options menu (File Manager), 50-51

P

parity, 145
Partial File Details (File Manager's View menu) command, 71, 72
Paste (Edit menu) command, 11
Paste Link (Edit menu) command, 92
Paste Special (Edit menu) command, 11, 92
pasting text, 10-11
 see also moving
patterns, background, 20
pausing printing, 121-122
 resuming, 123
PIF Editor
 386-Enhanced mode, 104-108
 Standard mode, 109-113
PIF files, 104
 DOS applications, 109
pointers, mouse, 98

ports
 COM
  options, 96
  settings, 145-146
 idle time, 96
 printers, selecting, 117-119
 serial, configuring, 145-147
Print (File menu) command, 121
Print Manager
 deleting jobs, 119-120
 window, 113
Printer (Options menu) command, 113
Printer Setup (File menu) command, 116
printers
 configuring, 113-115
 default, selecting, 116-117
 drivers, files, 116
 ports, selecting, 117-119
 settings, 113-115
Printers icon, 117
printing
 deleting jobs, 119-120
 files, 120-121
 pausing, 121-122
  resuming, 123
 priorities, 122-123
priorities, printing, 122-123
processors
 COM ports, 95
 sharing, 95
program groups
 adding, 124-126
 deleting, 126-127
 icons, 124
 items
  adding, 128-133
  creating icons, 128-133
  deleting, 133-134
  icon properties, 141-145
  moving, 135-136
 selecting icons, 86-87
 windows, selecting, 158

program item icons, 1
  adding to program group, 128-133
  creating, 128-133
  moving, 135-136
  properties, 141-145
  rearranging, 127
  selecting, 86-87
  starting programs, 128
program items, deleting, 133-134
Program Manager
  accessing with Task List, 125
  customizing, 127-159
  options, 127-128
  program groups
    adding, 124-126
    deleting, 126-127
    selecting windows, 158
  program item icons, properties, 141-145
  settings, saving, 127-128
  window, minimizing, 127
programs
  quitting, 136-137
  starting, 137-138
    program-item icons, 128
properties
  files, 138-141
    Archive, 141
    File Manager options, 138
    Hidden, 141
    Read Only, 141
    System, 141
  program item icons, 141-145
Properties (File menu) command, 139

Q

question mark (?) wild-card character
  renaming multiple files, 63-64
  searching for files, 67-68
Quit command, 136
quitting applications, 136-137

R

Read Only file property, 141
rearranging program-item icons, 127
Refresh (Window menu) command, 32
refreshing directory windows, 32-33
removing, see deleting
Rename (File Manager's File menu) command, 63-65
renaming files or directories, 62-65
Restore (Control menu) command, 157
restoring windows, 157
resuming paused printing, 123
Run (File Manager's File menu) command, 66

S

Save As (Clipboard Viewer's File menu) command, 12-13
Save Settings on Exit (File Manager's Options menu) command, 51, 128
saving
  Clipboard contents as files, 11-13
  settings, Program Manager, 127-128
screen savers, choosing, 20-21
screen elements, changing colors, 14-16
Search (File Manager's File menu) command, 67-68
searching for files, 67-68
Select Files (File Manager's File menu) command, 69
selecting
  files, 69-70
  icons, 86-87

printers
  default, 116-117
  ports, 117-119
  windows, 158
serial ports, configuring, 145-147
Set Up Applications (Setup's Options menu) command, 1-3
settings
  COM ports, 145-146
  printers, 113-115
  Program Manager, saving, 127-128
Settings (application's Control menu) command, 39-42
Setup applet
  choosing video drivers, 48-49
  installing Windows, 1-3
  system hardware settings, changing, 80-82
Setup dialog box, 45-47
sharing COM ports, 95
shortcut keys, suspending, 111
sizing windows, 158-159
Sort by Date (File Manager's View menu) command, 72
Sort by Name (File Manager's View menu) command, 72
Sort by Size (File Manager's View menu) command, 72
Sort by Type (File Manager's View menu) command, 72
sound cards, 147
sound drivers, 148
  installing, 44-47
sounds, configuring, 147-151
source documents (OLE), 92
  opening, 94
spacing, icons
  arranging automatically, 85
  setting, 21
Split (File Manager's View menu) command, 30-31
split bars, directory windows, 30

Standard mode, PIF Editor, 109-113
  options, 109-111
starting
  applications, 137-138
  Clipboard Viewer applet, 13-14
  File Manager, 52-53
  programs, 137-138
    program-item icons, 128
Status Bar (File Manager's Options menu) command, 51
stop bits, 145
subdirectories, *see* directories
suspending shortcut keys, 111
swap files, 97
Swap Left/Right Buttons (Control Panel), 98
Switch To (Control menu) command, 4-5
switching applications, 3-5
  fast switching, 20
system
  deleting fonts, 78-80
  hardware settings, changing, 80-82
System file property, 141

T

Task List, 150-151
  accessing Program Manager, 125
  changing applications, 150
  closing applications, 150
  switching applications, 4
terminating print jobs, 119-120
text
  copying or cutting to Clipboard, 6-7
  pasting from Clipboard, 10-11
Text (Clipboard Viewer's Display menu) command, 5-6

Tile (Window menu) command, 153
tiling windows, 150, 153
timeslices, 97
titles, icons, wrapping, 21
toggles, 73
   commands, 127
Tree and Directory (File Manager's View menu) command, 71
Tree Only (File Manager's View menu) command, 71
TrueType options, 151-152

U

Update (File menu) command, 103
updating
   directory-window contents, 32-33
   links, 93-95
      automatically, 93
   objects
      embedded, 102-103
      linked, 94
      locking, 94

V

VGA mode, displaying applications, 105
video drivers
   choosing, 48-49
   installing, 44-47
View menu (File Manager), 70-74
viewing
   Clipboard contents, 5-6
   directory contents, 25-26
   files, 70-75
virtual memory, 97

W-Z

wallpaper, choosing, 21
wild-card characters
   renaming multiple files, 63-64
   searching for files, 67-68
Windows
   adding applications, 1-3, 128-133
   background, 96
   documents, pasting to, 10-11
   foreground, 96
windows
   arranging, 152-153
   borders, setting widths, 21
   cascading, 150, 153
   closing applications, 153-154
   directory, selecting, 158
   maximizing, 154-155
   minimizing, 155-156
   moving, 156-157
   Print Manager, 113
   program groups, 124-126
      selecting, 158
   Program Manager, minimizing, 127
   restoring, 157
   selecting, 158
   sizing, 158-159
   tiling, 150, 153
Windows Setup icon, 1, 48, 80-81
wrapping icon titles, 21